INDECENT EXPOSURE

INDECENT EXPOSURE

A MEMOIR

PATRICK DODENHOFF

IngramSpark

Published by IngramSpark
Lavergne, TN

ISBN 979-8-218-14502-6

First Printing, 2023

This book is dedicated to my family who always stood by me and never gave up hope, especially to my mother who always told me to stay strong.

Prologue

"Hey, do you want to come over here and suck this for me?" My two friends and I were playing in the woods, looking for turtles and lizards, just doing what normal seven-year-olds did. We didn't see the guy until we were right up on him, about ten feet away. He was probably around thirty, white, and completely naked, sitting on an old tree that had fallen over. All three of us just froze in our tracks. I had never seen a grown man naked before. I had never seen anyone naked before. My eyes went right to his private parts. It was very big and shiny, with veins sticking out all around it, and his hand was rubbing on it up and down.

I couldn't move. All I could do was stand there and stare. What was he doing? Why was he out there? I was mesmerized. I don't know what made me stand there and watch him for so long, but as soon as he asked me if I wanted to touch it and suck it, something just clicked, and I said "no." We took off running as fast as we could out of the woods. I never did tell my mom.

I remember that day so clearly because my friends and I were playing with the new Bicentennial quarters that had just come out. It was 1976, and Gerald Ford was our president.

My mom loved to bowl, and she had her bowling trophies displayed all over the living room—hundreds of them. That morning she had to find a babysitter for me because she had to go bowling, so she got one of my friends' moms to watch me that day. So, it was just my two friends and me at the babysitter's house. We were all bored, so we asked my friend's mom if we could go play in the woods across the street. She said we could, just to be careful.

As we were leaving, I noticed a rug right inside the front door that was all crumpled up, so I reached down to straighten it out. My friend's mom saw me doing that and said, "You don't have to go play; you can stay here and help me clean if you want to."

"No, that's OK," I replied. "I would rather go play."

If only I could have known that going out to look for turtles and lizards was going to destroy my life, I would have stayed there and cleaned her entire house.

Today, I do not recall who my friends were; I wish I did because I would love to know if that incident had any impact on their lives like it had on mine.

So, here is my story. This is how a shy, innocent seven-year-old boy had his whole life destroyed by a man jacking off in the woods.

Chapter 1

If your family member is struggling with addiction,
Love them, don't fight them, don't judge them,
And for the love of everything holy, pray for them.
— Angela Davis

I was born on March 7, 1969, at Stoddard Memorial Hospital in Stoughton, Massachusetts. I lived in Massachusetts for the first two years of my life. My dad was a carpenter, and my mother was a stay-at-home mom. I had a brother who was two years older than me named Joey. We then moved to Pine Hills, Florida, where my mother gave birth to my two sisters, Ann-Marie then Kristie. We lived in Pine Hills for six years, which were the most impressionable years of my childhood.

My dad built a new roof on our house with a weird-looking border all around it that looked just like the roof of McDonald's, which made everybody laugh. We also had a big propane tank on the side of our house, and I would hide under it for hours, which freaked my mom out one time because she couldn't find me. So, she called the police, who found me hiding under the propane tank. I was four years old, and it was my first interaction with a police officer. It would not be my last.

My brother and I shared a room. Our curtains, sheets, blankets, and pillowcases all had baseball team logos on them. My mom had to put garbage bags on my mattress because I would pee the bed every night and would continue to do so for years.

My favorite things to play with were my Matchbox cars that I collected. I had a whole bunch of them, along with the cases to carry them around in. I also had a Tyco racetrack that I built by clipping the pieces together to make it in any shape I wanted. The cars had little magnets on the bottom, and you pressed a trigger on a hand-held gun to make the cars race around the track. I would play with that all day until one day, a girl that lived down the street came over and stole all the magnets. That was my first experience getting something stolen from me.

We didn't have a swimming pool, so I loved playing in the sprinklers. I also loved to build tents out of bedsheets in my bedroom and play with my cars under them.

I had my first girlfriend when I was six years old. Her name was Cinnamon, and she lived across the street. Cinnamon was cute; she had short brown hair, freckles all over her face, and looked just like Peppermint Patty.

One day she wanted to play doctor, but I was way too scared for that, so we would play in tents we built out of the sheets that were hanging from a clothesline. One day, while we were under there playing, my brother Joey was spying on us, trying to catch us doing something, and it just so happened that while he was looking in at us, I was reaching over Cinnamon to get something, and he automatically assumed we were kissing.

"You guys were kissing, you guys were kissing, I saw you kissing," Joey yelled.

We were not kissing, but Joey told my mom and everybody else he could think of in the neighborhood.

When I was seven, I got a brand-new bicycle. Back then, they had bikes with long seats called banana seats with sissy bars on the back of them; they were really cool. The first day I had it, I rode it over to the house of my mom's best friend, Candie. My mom was there, too, and I parked it in Candie's backyard, where she had two really big Great Danes. While I was in the house playing, the dogs chewed up my brand-new red banana seat, and there was sponge stuffing all over the place. Man, I cried so hard when I came out and saw that.

Candie's husband was a truck driver who brought his truck home from work every night. It was a really big Peterbilt that I was fascinated with from the first moment I saw it, which made me want to be a truck driver when I grew up. I'm sure my mom wasn't too happy about that career choice at such a young age. All my friends wanted to be doctors, lawyers, police officers, or firemen, but I wanted to be a truck driver.

I would go over there all the time just to look at his truck. He would take me inside and show me that the whole cab of the truck would tilt forward when he would check the engine. It was really cool and had a bed and it. Yep, that was what I was gonna be when I grew up—a truck driver.

My friends and I would ride our bikes all over the place. There was a YMCA we used to go to, but our favorite place to go was the Pine Hills Mall. We had a lot of fun there. They had a movie theater that we could sneak into. One of us would walk into the movie theater while the rest of us would wait outside by the fire exit door. We would open the door from the inside and go in and watch any movies we wanted for free. It was really easy to do, and we never got caught. I guess that was my first time ever doing any kind of mischief. Then we would look for glass bottles in the dumpsters and go smash them on the ground behind the mall. That was really fun. But the first time I ever stole anything was at a store called Belk Lindsey. They had these really cool rings that would change colors depending on your mood. I thought they were the greatest things ever. I'm not sure how many times I went in there, but I stole quite a few of them. They kept them right on the counter.

My childhood memories become more vivid after I turned seven. It was then that I remember seeing holes in the walls of our house and wondering how they got there. One day, I found out. I never heard my mom and dad fight or argue before, but one night I came into the dining room, and my dad was beating my mom's head into the wall. From that night on, I knew my dad was violent and would beat up my mom.

I also do not remember my dad ever doing anything with me. It seems like he was never around. The only real memory that I have of him having an old Triumph. It was a little convertible sports car that you had to crank start through the front grill. He would tell me to be careful of that crank because it could take my arm off. That's the only thing I ever remember learning from my dad.

My mom and dad must have been getting a divorce around that time. I knew something was going on because I never saw my dad again. He left my mom with four kids to raise on her own. It must've been very hard on my mom, but it was probably a relief for her to get rid of him. There's no telling how many times he had abused her.

My nana and grandpa came over a lot around that time. My grandmother had a '74 Oldsmobile Cutlass that was green with white leather interior that had the console and shifter in between the bucket seats. I loved that car.

My mom's sister Patricia, who we called Auntie Pat, would also come by and visit all the time. I didn't know what a lesbian was. I didn't even know anything about gay people, but I always thought there was something different about her. She always dressed like a boy. She had very short bleached-blonde hair and a man's wallet with a chain hooked to it. Her favorite T-shirt was a black one that said "BITCH" on the front. She was cool and always liked to wrestle with me, but I could never beat her because she was too strong.

There was an old man who lived behind us on the other side of the power lines that ran through an empty field behind our house. One day my sister Ann-Marie came home and told my mom that the old man touched her. Robert, a guy my mom was dating after my dad left, grew furious and threatened to run over there and kill him, but my mom stopped him or calmed him down because he never confronted the old man.

Chapter 2

My mother's divorce from my dad must have been finalized because she got married to Robert, who adopted my brother, two sisters, and me. Our last name was changed to his, and we moved to a city north of Orlando called Winter Springs in Seminole County, Florida. We settled into a nice house that was only a couple of years old. I think the main reason we all moved was that my mom was trying to keep us kids away from our real father. I could tell that she was very scared of him and was afraid he was going to come take us away from her. She always told us never to go anywhere with him if he ever showed up.

When she enrolled me into second grade at Winter Springs Elementary, she told my teachers and principal about my dad and to never under any circumstances let him pick up any of her kids from school for any reason. But she never had to worry about that because I never did see him again. He obviously didn't love me because he never came back or even tried to contact me. Oh well, I had a new dad that seemed to care about me. He worked for Coca-Cola and would bring me all kinds of cool Coke stuff: pens, pencils, and bottle caps that were not put on the bottles yet. I would peel the little round plastic off from underneath them and look for prizes—mostly for free sodas and money. We even had an old Coke machine in our garage that had the glass door you opened, then pulled the glass bottles out. It was really cool.

I was in second grade when I started liking girls, or at least I started paying more attention to them. A friend in my class asked me if I wanted to look up girls' dresses, then showed me how. Our classroom had a sink that was built into a countertop that extended from the wall that we could hide under, so when a girl used the sink, we could stick our heads out and look up their dresses.

I guess that's when I started to be a little pervert. But it wasn't my idea.

There was a girl named Melissa I had a crush on, but I was too shy to talk to her. I didn't know where she lived, but I always saw her walking home. So, one day I decided to follow her to see where she lived, hiding behind trees and cars so she wouldn't see me. I couldn't believe how far she walked to school every day; it was about two miles, which was a long way for a seven-year-old girl to walk. I didn't think I was doing anything weird at the time, just a normal seven-year-old boy who had a crush on the cutest girl at Winter Springs Elementary

My sisters Ann-Marie and Kristie loved Barbies. They had the Barbie dream house, motorhome, and Corvette. Sometimes I would play with them because I thought all that stuff was pretty cool, especially the motorhome. I would always be Ken. But my favorite thing of all was their Easy Bake Oven. I loved making little cakes I could eat. Those were pretty much the only toys of theirs I played with. One of my favorite games to play with my sisters was hide and seek; that was always fun too.

I did pretty good in school because when I finished second grade, my teacher said I could skip third grade if I wanted to, but my mom wouldn't let me. She didn't think it would be a good idea because I wouldn't be able to graduate with kids that were my age.

One day we had a show and tell at school. I don't remember what I brought. I think it might've been some Coca-Cola stuff. But I do remember what another kid in my class brought, and I sure wanted it. It was a really big penny from Walt Disney World that had Mickey Mouse on the front and the Magic Kingdom on the back. It was in a nice white velvet-lined box. The teacher left it on the base of the chalkboard, so I waited until nobody was looking during a break in class and stole it, then took it home and showed my mom, telling her I found it. She must have thought it was cool because she kept taking it from my room, and I would steal it back from her room.

My mom got pregnant by my step-dad and gave me a little brother, Bobby, who was his first child, named after him. We lived in a nice middle-class neighborhood right behind the elementary school. There were a lot of kids in the neighborhood to play with, so I had a lot of friends. *Star Wars* has just come out and was my favorite movie, so I collected *Star Wars* cards and all the action figures. I was a normal kid, doing what a normal kid did. I had two friends named Scott and John—at least I considered them my friends, but I didn't think they felt the same way about me, just a feeling I had. I thought they might have thought they were too good for me because they were a lot better in baseball than I was, and their dad was also the coach. I would play cowboys and Indians with them. They also had a swimming pool, so I would go over there and swim whenever I could. I also loved to ride my Big Wheel. I liked to hook a wagon to it and pretend I was driving a big semi with a trailer hooked to it. I would back into spots like I was delivering stuff. Yeah, I was going to be a truck driver someday.

Chapter 3

My nana and grandpa lived in Ponte Vedra Beach, Florida, where we would visit them once a month. One time, I stayed with them all by myself for a week, sleeping in their guest room, where it was always so quiet. All I could hear was the sound of their grandfather clock out in the hallway. I would also lay in bed and stare at a picture of Jesus they had hanging on the wall in that bedroom. I always felt that Jesus was staring at me, and it made me feel safe in there, like he was telling me not to worry, that he would protect me

One morning, my grandma told me we were going on a trip to Mobile, Alabama. I asked her why we were going there, and she asked if I knew who Jimmy Buffett was. I said, "no." She said we were going to his house. So, we drove all the way there in her brand-new green Cutlass. She bought a new Oldsmobile every year.

When we arrived in Mobile at a high-rise condominium, I never did see or meet Jimmy Buffett, but I did meet an older lady who was my grandma's age; she must have been Jimmy Buffett's mother and was good friends with my grandma. I saw gold framed records all over the walls, but to this day, I have no idea how they met and became friends.

My grandpa ended up meeting us there later that night. I brought my Matchbox car collection so I would have something to play with. That first night they all decided to go out, so they hired a babysitter to watch me. My grandpa promised me before he left that he would bring me back a Matchbox car for my collection, so I was very excited and couldn't wait for him to come back to see what new car he was going to bring me. I waited up all night for them, and when they finally got back early the following morning, my grandpa didn't have the new car for me. I was devastated. But he did teach me a very good lesson that I never forgot. If you tell someone you are going to do something, you better fucking do it, especially a little kid, because they will remember. I believe seven, eight, nine, and ten are the most crucial ages in kids' minds; that's when they really remember things that stay with them for the rest of their lives.

On the way home from Mobile, from Jimmy Buffett's parents' house, I slept in the backseat with no seatbelt on because I was lying from side to side. My grandmother was hauling ass, and the next thing I knew, I was woken up by a cop talking to her through the passengers' window on the side of Interstate-10. She got pulled over for speeding and was trying to talk her way out of the ticket. I remember hearing the cop say, "Ma'am, I wrote so many tickets, I could fill up a Sears Catalog." Then I heard my grandma say she was just trying to beat a previous time set by my grandpa from mobile to Ponte Vedra Beach. The cop said "hi" to me, wrote my Nana a speeding ticket, then left.

I wish I knew more about my grandparents. I loved going to their house because they had a swimming pool and let me eat anything I wanted. I love their mixed nuts I had to crack myself, cookies, and sherbet ice cream, but their favorite, diet Tab soda, tasted like shit. I could tell they really loved me. They were both retired from the navy; maybe that's where they met the Buffets.

My grandfather loved making clocks out of cypress trees. I enjoyed watching him make them in his woodshop. He would always give me pens and mechanical pencils that said "US Government" on them. I had a lot of good memories of my trips to their house. I also remember them being very scared because their house had been burglarized—not only once, but twice. My grandfather was very worried because one of the times my grandmother was home alone, and the burglars were watching her through her bedroom window getting dressed for work. The police found the spot where they were hiding right outside her bedroom window. The burglars also painted a gold tooth on a donkey planter they had in the kitchen, which was really weird. After that second burglary, they moved to a new house in Edgewater, Florida.

Chapter 4

I really love baseball. When I was ten, my mom signed me up for T-ball. There was a baseball park not far from our house called Five Points. All the leagues were named after horses. The T-ball league was called Pinto, then Mustang, Bronco, Pony, and Colt. Then you would go on to play in high school if you were good enough and had good grades. I made it all the way to Pony. I was a catcher in Pinto, then went on to play mostly outfield and occasionally first base. I really sucked. I was never good at all, but I really enjoyed playing. My neighbors Scott and John were also my age and played all the leagues with me but were a lot better than I was and went on to play in high school.

One time, my mom took me shopping at a sporting goods store to buy me a new glove. This was not long after she had another baby, my sister Stacie who came out with bright orange hair. Nobody knew where her red hair came from. The guy who delivered potato chips to our house every week didn't have red hair, neither did the mailman. So, I guess she was from my stepdad, which was her dad; he did have a reddish tint to his beard. Stacie is the only redhead in our family; the rest of us all have brown hair and brown eyes.

Anyway, we were in the sporting goods store, and I saw a glove that I really wanted. It was a Mizuno that cost $75. My mom tried to tell me that it was too expensive and she couldn't afford that much, but I started crying and insisted on that glove. She tried to show me a more reasonable Rawlings at a much lower price, but I wasn't listening. I just kept crying until she got it for me. It was even too big, but my thinking was that I would be able to catch better with it because it was bigger. I felt bad for being so selfish. I knew she didn't have much money because she was trying to raise six kids. To make matters worse, on the very first game I used it, I was in the Bronco League playing left field, and a fly ball was hit right to me. I caught it, but my glove fell off with the ball still in it because my glove was too big. That was the most embarrassing moment of my life up until that point. I felt like such an idiot, and it was during a big game with all the parents watching. My stepdad never went to any of my games, but my mom would go to every one of them.

I was also getting into BMX bikes around that time. My first one was a black Huffy with yellow mag wheels I got for Christmas. My brother Joey and I both got one that year. My stepdad loved to surprise us on Christmas. He would ask me if I would go out and get the newspaper for him out in the driveway, and I would go, and my new bike would be sitting right there. He would love to surprise us like that.

He had quit working at Coca-Cola and started working as a salesman for a coffee company. He would drive a van around to different cities and sell coffee machines and coffee to businesses. One day, he took me on a trip to Arcadia, Florida, with him. He had a CB radio in his van that I thought was the coolest thing. He would let me talk on it, and he showed me how it worked. Once, I heard a woman talk dirty to him on the CB. My dad told her to be careful because he had little ears with him, referring to me.

My dad would also take Joey and me to watch professional wrestling at a place called Eddie Graham Sports Stadium in Orlando. It was before wrestling got really big with the WWF and WWE. I saw Dusty Rhodes, Ric Flair, Barry, and Kendall Wyndham, Chief Wahoo McDaniel, and a bunch of others. It was really exciting. We went quite a few times. One night my dad got kicked out of the stadium because he hit a wrestler named Kevin Sullivan. Kevin said something to my dad, and my dad hit him and was escorted out of the stadium. My dad told us we could stay and meet him at the car when it was over.

My dad had a lot of different salesman-type jobs. He quit working at the coffee company and started working for a company selling machines. I don't know what they were, but he would come home with these big-ass machines on the back of his truck that he would drive around to different companies and try to sell them for commission. He only had that job for about a month or two; then he got a job working at a used car lot. I enjoyed that because he would always bring a different cool car home every night. I loved how he would always fool my mom by bringing home a really nice Corvette or Nissan 280 ZX and tell my mom they were for her, and she would get all excited; then he would tell her he was just kidding. It was so mean, but it was funny.

When my sister Stacie was born, he rented one of those big flashing advertising signs that had a huge arrow on top that would point toward the business you are advertising. It came with plastic letters, so you could write whatever you wanted on it. He put it in our front yard so my mom would see it when she came home from the hospital. It said, "Welcome home mommy and Stacie Lynn."

My dad was also into old cool stuff. He bought an old pinball machine and bumper pool table for our garage along with that old Coke machine. So, we had the cool house where kids liked to come over and play. We also had a train set that took up half our garage. It had an entire city with trees, people, houses, mountains, and bridges. That was fun to play with. Through my dad, I learned to love things like vintage slot machines, jukeboxes, pool tables, Coke machines, anything old like that, even classic cars. My dad loved them, too. Once, he bought a T-bucket, then traded that for a '56 Chevy Bel Air, then traded that for '34 Ford. He also had a dune buggy.

The last job I remember my dad having was as a tire salesman. His father owned El Dorado tires, so I'm sure that's why my dad got into that business. He knew a lot about tires and was really good at that job because he did it for a long time and eventually owned his own tire business.

Chapter 5

I had two friends, Scott and John, whose dad took to us to see the Tampa Bay Buccaneers play the Minnesota Vikings when Doug Williams was the quarterback for Tampa. It was the first football game I ever went to. My dad asked if I could get him a program from the game. I didn't know what that was but told him I would get him one. Tampa Bay wasn't that good and ended up losing that game. On our way out of the stadium, I asked my friends' dad if I could get a program to take back for my dad.

"Why didn't you say something earlier?" their dad asked.

"I didn't know," I replied.

He then said it was too late and we wouldn't be able to find one. I was so upset because I felt like I was letting my dad down. I didn't say another word all the way back to Winter Springs.

My friends and I loved to play Nerf football in the street in front of my house. We would alternate between playing that or baseball. But instead of using a real baseball, we had to use a tennis ball to keep from breaking any windows. We could only play until the streetlights came on. Then we all had to go home. Also, around that time, a truck would drive through the neighborhood spraying for mosquitoes, and we didn't want to be out there when he drove by.

My brothers, sisters, and I had a lot of toys and games between us. We would get together every Saturday night and have a family game night, which I really looked forward to. My mom loved to play board games and cards. Our favorite games to play on that night were Rummy 500, Sorry, and Yahtzee. We had Monopoly, but I hated that fucking game because it took too long to play. Other card games we played included Crazy Eights, War, Slapjack, and Go Fish. That was always a fun night. We also had an Atari video game system that had a lot of cool games on it that I loved to play, like Space Invaders, Asteroids, Frogger, and Pac-Man. I also had a Stretch Armstrong, which was a muscleman doll that you could pull on and stretch really far. One day I got curious and wondered what was inside of him to make him be able to do that, so I got a knife out of the kitchen drawer and cut him open, and saw there was a bunch of jelly stuff inside. My curious mind wanted to know.

My friends and I would ride our bikes to the local Stop-N-Go convenience store and play their video games. That was also when I started stealing again. I would steal mostly fireballs, Jolly Ranchers, and baseball cards. We would also go over to a store right down the street from there called Joe's Meat Market because in the back of that store was a small fenced-in area where they kept all the empty returnable glass bottles. We would jump the fence and steal as many bottles as we could carry, then take them right back in the front door and return them for five and ten cents apiece, then buy candy. Then we would ride our bikes to a place called Ice Cream Castle and buy ice cream, or go to another store called Cumberland Farms and look for different kinds of candy to buy.

During the summer months, we would go to a place called Wekiva Falls/Rock Springs and rent big tractor-tire inner tubes to float down a stream with, which was really fun. We would float to the end where they had a boardwalk that led back to the beginning; then we would do it again.

The first time I went there, I saw a woman in a bathing suit, and I was surprised to discover that she had hair "down there." I think she was a lifeguard, but I wasn't sure. She was at the end of the stream, standing by the railing of the boardwalk. She was in her twenties, with long blonde hair and wearing a green one-piece bathing suit. She was really pretty, so I was staring at her body and saw a lot of blonde hairs sticking all out of the sides of her bathing-suit bottom. I guess shaving wasn't popular back then because she had a real hairy pussy, but she was sexy as hell, so I hurried and got back to the beginning of the stream so I could go back down and look at her again.

The first time I ever heard a girl cuss, besides on the CB, was when we went to a place called Turkey Lake Park that had a nice lake for swimming. There was a girl who was around eighteen, arguing with someone.

I heard her yell, "I don't give a flying fuck!" That stuck with me because I wasn't allowed to cuss. My mom always taught me not to, and I never did. The first time I ever cussed, I was eighteen and did it by accident in front of my mom.

Summertime was fun. When we weren't going to different places, I would usually find someone with a swimming pool, usually Scott and John's house, or I would play on my Slip-N-Slide. We also had an ice cream truck that came by our house, along with a Polar Cup guy who sold lemon-flavored sno-cones. There were a lot of kids in my neighborhood, so there was always something to do.

Chapter 6

My mom got pregnant again. I remember her favorite shirt said, "Practice makes perfect, I should know." She would also play a song on her record player called *Pregnant Again*.

Now I had another little sister; her name was Stephanie. My mom now had seven kids: four by my real father and three by my stepdad.

My mom enrolled me at All Souls Catholic school in Sanford, Florida. I was raised Catholic, so my mom would make me go to mass every Sunday, which I fucking hated. It was so boring, but I put up with it just for the free donuts they gave away at the end of the services. My dad would never go with us; he would stay at home to do yard work and drink beer.

In the fourth grade, I would take a bus on the way to Sanford from Winter Springs. My bus stop was at the Automotive 1 auto parts store right next to the Stop-N-Go. My bus driver was in his 80s, and one day he never showed up to take me to school, so I stayed home and found out the following day that he was found dead in the school parking lot on the morning he was supposed to pick me up. He had a heart attack. All the kids were lucky that he didn't die while we were all on the bus. I ended up getting a ride to school from Scott and John's mom for about a week after that until they could find another bus driver.

I was extremely shy all throughout school, especially during my time at All Souls. I had a nun for a teacher in one of my classes, and I would never say a word in class, so she ended up calling my mom and asking her if I was a deaf-mute. I was scared to go to school on Fridays because that was when they had confession, and I would have to sit in a booth and confess my sins to a priest, which terrified me. I wouldn't say a word. I would just sit there until the priest told me I could leave. I went to All Souls for a couple of years, and not once did I say a word in that confession booth. I would always pretend I was sick on Fridays, just so I wouldn't have to go to confession. I dreaded it.

I was even too shy to excuse myself from the dinner table at home after eating. I would sit there for a long time because I couldn't say, "May I be excused?"

It was also at All Souls in the fifth grade where I learned to be a businessman. I would go to the Stop-N-Go that later became a Circle K and bought a whole bunch of Life Savers that were ten cents a pack; then I would bring them to school and sell them for twenty-five cents a pack and made a fifteen-cent profit on each one. I was doing big things. I would average $1.50 a day doing that. I was a little entrepreneur.

I also had to wear a uniform to school: navy-blue pants and a white shirt. The girls would wear plaid skirts with white button-down shirts. That, I would later on discover, was sexy as hell.

A girl named Katie had a big-time crush on me. We rode the same bus, and she would always give me notes with dollar bills inside of them. She was really cute, with blonde hair and blue eyes, but she had some kind of sleeping disease. Every time her head would tilt to a certain side, she would fall asleep, so she was always asleep on the bus.

I was too shy to have a girlfriend, so I was afraid to talk to her.

A friend's mother who went to school there with me had a Trans Am just like the one from *Smokey and the Bandit*, which was my favorite movie at the time. She would pick him up and drop him off at school every day. Man, I loved that car; it was black with the gold eagle on the hood, with T tops. Man, I wanted to have a car like that someday.

My favorite TV shows were the *Dukes of Hazard* and *B.J. and the Bear*.

We used to play a game on the bus going to and from school that was really fun called Beetle. Every time you saw a Volkswagen bug, you would say "Beetle" and get one point. If you saw a Volkswagen bus, you would say "Beetle Beetle" and get two points. Then, whoever had the most points by the time we got to school would be the winner. Back then, there were a lot of Volkswagens on the road. I would get about twelve of them on the way to school.

One day in class, the nun told everyone that whoever was the best behaved that day would get a prize. I really wanted to win, so every moment that I was sitting at my desk and not using my hands, I had them neatly folded on my desk in front of me while looking straight ahead and perfectly still. I did that all day and still didn't win; I was so devastated because I knew I was the best behaved. The teacher obviously wasn't paying attention, because I should have won. So, from that day on, I never even tried to win that stupid contest.

They also had a show-and-tell at All Souls, and I had brought my Frisbee. It wasn't just any Frisbee; it was a real professional one given to me by a professional Frisbee player; I loved that thing. It was big and flew far. You couldn't buy one like it at Kmart or a sporting goods store. During recess that day, my friend and I were throwing it, and it ended up on the roof of one of the classrooms. So, I went and told the teacher, and she said there was nothing she could do, so I couldn't get it back. Man, I was mad; I couldn't believe it. I cried for a long time. Maybe that was the karma I got for stealing that Walt Disney World penny from Winter Springs Elementary during their show-and-tell.

Chapter 7

The first time a girl tried to do something sexual with me, I was playing at Winter Springs Elementary. It was only a block away from my house, so I would go there and play a lot. There was a girl there who was a little older than me. I was nine or ten, and she was twelve or thirteen and lived in the neighborhood behind the Piggly Wiggly supermarket about a mile away. We were playing together, and she wanted to walk around the school with me. The school was round, and there were doors to every classroom all around the school, and each door had a little breezeway in front of it that offered privacy.

So we were just hanging out in one of those breezeways in the back of the school, and she told me to lay down on my back. So I did, then she grabbed at my pants and was trying to undo the button and pull down my zipper. I jumped up and asked what she was doing.

"I want to see your thing," she said.

Man, I was so terrified, I ran all the way home.

The next time I saw her after that was a few years later in high school, and she had a nice fucking body. It was also the time I was really starting to get into girls, and all I could think of, was, *Wow! I fucked up.* Here was this sexy-ass girl that just a few years earlier wanted to see my thing and play with it, and no telling what else, and I ran like hell. I never did get to have sex with her. But I'm sure she found plenty of guys who weren't as scared of her as I had been.

Chapter 8

I really enjoyed working on and fixing BMX bikes. I loved to take them apart, clean them, and put them back together from all the parts my friends and I would find. I wanted to be a BMX racer. I would put a number plate on my bike, with racing stickers all over it, and ride my bike everywhere. I would ride to a bike shop called Bicycle Castle and look at all the really cool racing bikes they had. They had Redlines, GTs, and Mongooses. I couldn't afford any of those, so I would just look at them, then buy BMX stickers to stick all over my bike, then my friend Robert and I would ride to the Altamonte Mall to hang out and look in all the stores and do crazy stuff.

It was a typical two-story mall, so we would go up to the second floor and drop small stuff on people down on the first floor, then take off running. We would mostly drop pennies and thought that was the funniest thing.

They had a novelty store called Spencer's that was our favorite; they had a lot of cool stuff in there.

Then we would ride our bikes all the way back to Winter Springs, which was a long bike ride.

There was a BMX track that someone built by my house that Robert and I would go to all the time. It had a really big jump. One day while we were there, I hit that jump as fast as I could and crash-landed on my back, and got the wind knocked out of me. I couldn't breathe, and I got really scared because I thought I was going to die. It was the scariest feeling in the world when I was trying to breathe but couldn't, so I was glad Robert was with me because, for some reason, he punched me in the stomach, thinking it would help me breathe. It worked because I finally started breathing again.

I was a big-time daredevil. I loved to make ramps out of wood and jump them with my bike. They weren't small ramps either; they were really big ones. I would have to get a block away just so I could build up enough speed to jump them. I would line up garbage cans, and even neighborhood kids would lay on the ground so I could jump over them. I would line up ten garbage cans and just fly over them. I had no fear. I even had some pretty big wipeouts. One time I landed so hard on my front tire that my handlebars stripped out, and I did a faceplant. So, I always made sure my landings were in the grass, just for that reason. When I was jumping, they were always big spectacles. All the neighborhood kids would come over to watch me. I would even get my mom to come out and watch. I wanted to be just like Evel Knievel when I grew up.

I also loved to climb trees. I would look for the biggest, highest trees I could find and climb to the top of them without any fear; and they were really big trees. The hardest part was climbing down. Then I moved on to climbing powerlines, which was probably a lot more dangerous than climbing trees. When I climbed the powerlines, I could see all the high-rise buildings in downtown Orlando from Winter Springs. I'm sure I would have been arrested if I was ever caught doing that.

Then one day, I got the bright idea to jump off my next-door neighbor's roof with an umbrella to see if it would work because I saw it on *Mary Poppins*. I found out really quick that it didn't. The umbrella turned inside out, and I hit the ground really hard and thought for sure that I had broken my legs. The umbrella didn't even slow me down at all.

I guess this was when I became an adrenaline junkie. But nothing would compare to the ultimate adrenaline rush I would discover at the age of fourteen. I would never jump ramps, climb trees, or powerlines ever again.

Then I moved on to less-crazy stunts. I had a skateboard and would look for big hills, then sit on the skateboard and go down really fast, or I would get inside a big tractor tire and roll down hills in that. That was crazy because the tire would get rolling pretty fast, and I wouldn't be able to stop it. I would get really dizzy, so I only tried that once.

It didn't snow in Central Florida, so we never had snowball fights; we had acorn fights. We would gather up all the acorns that fell off the trees and throw them at each other. We would also put them in slingshots and shoot each other.

We had plants in Florida we called sticker bushes because when you walked through them, they would stick all over you. They would get stuck all in your shoelaces. There were sharp thorny little things that we would also throw at each other because they would stick to your clothes. You had to pull them out of the ground by the stems so they wouldn't poke you. We also had rock fights, but they had to be little rocks so we wouldn't kill each other.

Chapter 9

Growing up with six brothers and sisters, we had a big backyard that bordered the woods, so we had room for all kinds of animals, including a hen named Henrietta that laid brown eggs every morning. We also had chickens, roosters, rabbits, fish, turtles, hamsters, gerbils, snakes, hermit crabs, parakeets, lizards, dogs, cats, guinea pigs, you name it, we had it. We had a miniature zoo in our backyard. I would find all the turtles, lizards, and snakes out in the woods behind our house.

I loved hunting in the woods. My mom wouldn't let me have a BB gun until I was fourteen years old, but I would catch all the gopher turtles I could and save them as pets. Sometimes my dog, Sheba, would go hunting with me. She was a black lab, German shepherd mix, and when she saw a turtle go into its hole, she would go crazy and dig frantically, trying to get to it, but would eventually give up.

I also love to build forts in the woods. I'm sure I got my real father's genes because he was a carpenter. Back in those days, people would just dump all their trash and junk in the woods, so I would find all kinds of stuff to build my forts with. I would build really elaborate two- and three-story ones, with secret trapdoors and carpet. I would spend all day out there hammering away. I really enjoyed being out there by myself doing that. I spent a lot of time in the woods, wandering around looking for stuff to put in my forts.

There was a kid named Mark who lived in an old farmhouse in the woods. He was a couple of years older than me, and he and I became friends. One day I went over to his house, and he showed me his bedroom, and I couldn't believe what I saw. He had magazine pictures of naked women hung up all over his walls. Wow! I was mesmerized by them. They were all beautiful, grown women, and I asked him, "Your mom lets you hang these in your room?" It was my first time seeing naked women.

I also had a friend who lived across the street from me named Kimberly. She wasn't my girlfriend, but we would hang out in my fort and play board games. One day I was telling her about all the naked-girl pictures Mark had in his bedroom, and she said she found a magazine in her mom and dad's bedroom and asked if I wanted to go look at it when her mom and dad went to work. Her dad had it hidden in his dresser drawer, so we went and looked at it, which was the second time in a week that I was exposed to porn.

Chapter 10

One day, I was out looking for wood and saw a very nice piece tangled up in a palmetto bush, so I went to reach for it, stepped in a big hole, and fell. That's when I realized I stepped in a nest of yellowjacket wasps. There were hundreds of them all over my face and body, stinging me. I thought I was going to die.

I started to run home as fast as I could while screaming and trying to get them off me. I was swatting and wiping them off my face and arms, yelling for help. I had never been so scared in my life. Thank God my mom was home and saw what had happened and started pulling all the stingers out of me. I can't remember exactly how many she pulled out, but it was over forty. Then she put medicine on me, and I stayed in bed for two days. But when I woke up, my eyes were completely swollen shut.

From that day on, I've been terrified of bees and wasps. I don't want to get stung by them ever again. I was also a lot more careful where I stepped when I was in the woods after that.

I had just turned fourteen and was finally allowed to have a BB gun. So every time I went into the woods, I always brought that with me, even though it wouldn't protect me from wasps. I loved to shoot lizards, squirrels, and birds.

We lived in a four-bedroom house, so my older brother Joey and I shared a room, my sisters Ann-Marie and Kristie shared one, my brother Bobby and sisters Stacie and Stephanie shared one, and my mom and dad had their own room, so you can imagine all the chaos there was.

Just normal fighting that brothers and sisters did, but for the most part, we got along pretty good. The main problem I had with my sisters, especially Kristie, was that she would always tell on me for everything, mainly over me eating something I wasn't supposed to.

My mom loved Little Debbie snack cakes and had a whole cabinet full of Swiss Rolls, Nutty Bars, Oatmeal Pies, and every other kind of cake that Little Debbie made. My mom didn't like us going in there and stealing them, but I would every chance I got, and my sister Kristie would always come out of nowhere and catch me, and always say, "Ooohh, I'm telling," then run right to my mom and snitch me out on the spot. She would tell on me for everything. If she saw me with my hand in the cookie jar, she would run and tell, if she saw me getting an ice cream sandwich out of the freezer, she would run and tell. I had to wait until she was completely out of the house before I could take anything. She was something else.

My mom also loved Whitman's chocolates, the ones in the yellow box, which she kept in her bedroom. I would always sneak in there when she was at work and steal them, but first, I would take little bites out of them to make sure they were the good ones with dark brown in the middle. If they had orange, red, or white cream, I would leave them in the box and only eat the good ones. Sorry, mom, that was me who stole your chocolates and left little bites in the rest of them.

I also did something to my sisters that I knew they hated. I would chase them, and when I caught them, I would get them down on the ground on their backs and sit on their stomachs and stick my hands in their armpits and tickle them. Then I would pin their arms down and fart on them while I was sitting on their chest. They would scream, yell, and start crying, then go tell on me.

Me and my brother Joey, now that was a whole different story. He would always beat me up until one day, I finally got tired of it. He hit me so hard while we were in the kitchen, I ran to the kitchen drawer and grabbed a pair of those big-ass scissors with the orange plastic handles, and he took off running around the kitchen table, so I threw the scissors at him, and he ducked just in time, because right when he ducked, the scissors stuck in the wall where his head would've been. So from that day on, every time he hit me, he would take off running because he knew I was going to pick up the nearest thing I could find and hit him with it.

Chapter 11

When I was fourteen, I was too young to get a job, but I was always looking for ways to make money because I wanted to be able to buy cool racing parts for my bike, baseball cards, and other stuff. So I started mowing lawns. I started with our lawn because it was one of the chores that I had to do, besides cleaning my room and taking out the garbage. I would go around and knock on all the neighbors' doors and ask them if they would like their lawns mowed. I would charge $5 a lawn, but if they had a big lawn, I would charge them $8. I mowed quite a few lawns every week. I always did a really good job and built up a nice little business. I loved doing that. It was fun, especially when I was making about $40 a week, which was a lot for me at that age.

I also got a job as a Junior Salesman selling candy. There was a guy that would pick a bunch of us kids up in a van and drive us around to different cities and neighborhoods. We each had to carry a box full of assorted candies, cookies, chocolates, peanut brittle, saltwater taffy, and caramel clusters. He would drop us off, then pick us up at a certain spot, reload us back up, and send us out again.

"Hi, my name is Patrick, and I am a member of Junior Salesman, whose main goal is to keep teenagers busy and out of trouble."

Well, that was the speech I was supposed to give, but never did, because I was too shy to say it. All that I would say was, "Do you want to buy some candy?"

The boss would also give a bonus to the best salesman of the day. I didn't do that job for very long because I made a lot more money mowing lawns, so I preferred that.

Chapter 12

My mom loved ceramics and ran a ceramic business out of our garage. She made all kinds of things, especially around the holidays, like Christmas trees, Halloween pumpkins, and just about everything else you could imagine. She had hundreds of molds for making different things and two kilns, ovens used to harden the ceramic pieces once they were taken out of the molds. I helped her scrape and sand down the seams that showed after the pieces were taken out of the molds. I also helped her paint. She did pretty well and had a big contract making pots for a florist shop in the Altamonte Mall. Our garage was completely full of ceramic stuff at one time.

My mom also worked at a convenience store called Winter Springs Beverage Barn, which was a drive-thru store on Highway 434, right across the street from Big Cypress golf course, which was less than a mile from our house. It was a pretty cool store because people wouldn't have to get out of their cars. All they had to do was just drive up and order whatever they wanted—mostly beer, cigarettes, milk, bread, or sodas, and my mom would bring it right up to their windows.

I loved going there and helping her stock the freezer and straighten up the shelves. She always gave me candy and sodas in return.

Chapter 13

I started getting into golf because my dad had a set of golf clubs in the garage, so I used them to practice in the backyard. I would also go to the elementary school to see how far I could hit them.

I had a friend named Darren who also liked to play, so he would always come over, and we would go to the driving range at Big Cypress golf course and hit balls. I enjoyed it so much, my mom enrolled me into junior golf lessons at a golf course in Casselberry, the next city over from Winter Springs. They had a professional golfer who taught the classes. It was fun; then, they held a tournament for all the students at the end of the lessons. I can't remember what place I came in, but I know it wasn't first because I wasn't that good. My mom even got me a subscription to *Golf Digest* for my birthday that year.

The only sports that I enjoyed growing up were baseball, golf, and Frisbee. I'm not sure if Frisbee is a sport, but I enjoyed it.

Chapter 14

I was very shy in school and never really felt that I fit in. I didn't hang out in groups and didn't really have any friends. I pretty much kept to myself. The only kids I knew were the kids who lived in my neighborhood, but they really weren't my friends. I called them my friends, but they weren't.

I probably weighed 100 pounds in middle school, so I would get picked on a lot, especially in gym class. For some reason, I was terrified to wear shorts because I had the skinniest, whitest legs and didn't want anyone to see them. I didn't even wear shorts at home, so I would be terrified to go to gym class because we were supposed to change into shorts, and I would always refuse. You'd think I would've worn shorts, growing up in Florida, but for some reason, I was just too shy and embarrassed to wear them. I refused for a whole year before the coach finally called me into his office and told me that I had to wear them or he would have to fail me. So, that scared me enough to bring shorts to school the following day, which was the most terrifying day of my life. But I went, and it was the most humiliating experience of my life. Kids made fun of me and laughed, even mocking my name. I never wanted to go to gym class ever again.

It wasn't called bullying back then, but that's exactly what it was. I really got picked on a lot after that day. The thing that terrified me the most was when one of the bigger kids would pick a fight with me at school, then tell me to wait until after school when we got off the bus. Man, I hated when that happened because then I would have to go through the whole day just knowing I was gonna get beat up after school. Now, that was the worst feeling ever, and I had no friends to help me, so that really scared me because I didn't like to fight; plus, I didn't even know how, so that was always a very traumatizing experience.

There was this one kid who I thought was my friend. His name was Robert. He was on my baseball team and his dad was also a coach. But I knew Robert would only hang out with me when his cooler friends were not around.

We were both just getting into go-karts and minibikes, so we would get together and work on them. One time, we rode our go-karts all the way from Winter Springs to a flea market in Sanford without getting stopped by the police.

We would also go to a place called Little 500, where you could race go-karts around a track. They even had a gigantic slide that was about five stories high, so we liked going there.

Robert and I started doing some really crazy stuff together. One day, we broke into Winter Springs Elementary through the roof. We just climbed on the roof and discovered a secret trapdoor that led into the school; We couldn't believe it. So, we waited until that night to break in. We stole candy, pens, and pencils from all the teachers' desks. We were big-time burglars.

One time, we got caught on the roof by a guy who ended up chasing us to the edge, and we had no choice but to jump. But the guy chasing us was too scared to jump, and we got away. We then ran to a kid's house who lived right behind the elementary school and hid in his garage. We were really scared. Then, after about twenty minutes of hiding in the garage, we came out and there was a cop walking beside the house looking for us, and we took off running again. Oh my God, I couldn't believe it, the cop was telling us to freeze, but we kept on running. He then told us to stop or he would shoot, but we kept running anyway; there was no way I was stopping and getting caught for breaking into a school. I was out of there.

Robert and I both got away that day and never thought about going into that school ever again. But we never stopped doing crazy stuff.

Another funny thing we loved to do was make road-blocks. There were two factory warehouses behind my house through the woods. One factory was called Afcom, where they made nuts and bolts, and the other factory was called Continental Circuits, which made circuit boards, and there was only one road through the woods leading to both of those places. So Robert and I would drag all kinds of stuff out of the woods and onto the road when no cars were coming. We would drag out logs, tree branches, old tires, and whatever else we could find. We even strung fishing line across the street from tree to tree. Then we would hide in the woods where nobody could see us and wait for a car to come by. That was so fucking fun and would make us laugh so hard, until one day we did it to the wrong guy, who actually saw us dragging stuff out onto the road, so we took off running and heard him slam on his brakes, jump out of his truck, and start chasing us. He was fucking pissed. We thought he was really gonna kill us. He chased us through the woods all the way to the elementary school, which was a long way, before he finally gave up.

I was on the track team at South Seminole, but I was really glad he gave up because I was getting tired fast. We got away and never did another roadblock again.

When we got back to my house, we decided to ride our bikes to an arcade in Fern Park to play video games. I don't know if I was a bad influence on Robert or he was a bad influence on me.

Chapter 15

There was a sand and gravel place out on Highway 419, about five miles away from my house, so one day, Robert and I decided to ride our bikes over there on a Sunday when they were closed to see what kind of trouble we could get into. It was his idea, so I think he was a bad influence on me.

We jumped the fence when we got there and headed straight for the office, which we broke into, to see what we could find. We hit the jackpot when we found a couple of porn magazines, then a set of keys that fit all the tractors and bulldozers that were there.

Then we went out, and each got in a tractor and drove all over that place. It was so much fun; we had the greatest time. We were crashing into each other, then crashed into the office. We did that for over an hour before we decided we'd better get the hell out of there. We took the porn magazines with us and never went back because we made one hell of a mess.

But I ended up going back all by myself for a whole different reason, which I will get into later.

Chapter 16

There was a girl named Cindy who lived five houses down from me who I was really in love with. She had blonde hair, blue eyes and would end up becoming my girlfriend. But I was too damn shy to even think about doing anything with her.

They had a carnival come to our town; actually, it was the next town over, in Casselberry. It was in the parking lot of the Greyhound dog track. So, I asked Cindy if she wanted to go there with me, and she said yes, which was actually my first real date with a girl. It was close enough that we were able to ride our bikes there.

Once we got there, we locked our bikes up and started walking, looking at all the rides and games. While we were walking, I noticed our hands kept bumping into each other. I knew she was doing it on purpose, trying to hint to me to hold her hand, but I was too scared and terrified to do it. That's how shy I was. Then, after one too many times, she finally just grabbed my hand and made me hold hers, and that was it; we then held hands the rest of the time we were there.

On our way home, she wanted to play a game and asked if I wanted to play. I said. "Okay." While we were riding our bikes through the neighborhoods, she said she would touch people's mailboxes, and every time she touched a mailbox, it would mean a word, and I had to try and guess what she was saying.

"Okay, let's go." She then touched six mailboxes in a row. I had no idea what she was trying to say. I just knew it was six words, so I told her to give me a clue on the first word, and she said, "I." And she hit five more, and I still couldn't guess what she was trying to say, so I said, "I give up," and that's when she told me the answer, while she did it all over again with the next six mailboxes.

She hit the first one and said, "I," hit the second one and said. "wish," hit the third one and said "I," hit the fourth and said "could," the fifth and said, "kiss," and finally touched the last one and said, "you."

I was speechless. I didn't know what to say. I didn't say another word until we got to her house.

When we got to her house, we were hanging out in her driveway, and she was very close to me; I knew what she wanted to do, and I made up an excuse really quick that I was late for dinner or something like that, and got the hell out of there as fast as I could.

So, that was how my first date went.

Chapter 17

Going to the skating rink was really popular and fun. We had a skating rink called Semoran Skateway that I started going to every weekend. Cindy and I would go, and I would always look forward to the couples-only songs so we could go out on the floor together and hold hands. I was a terrible skater, but I sure had fun.

The most popular song that everyone would get all excited about was a song called *You Dropped a Bomb on Me* by The Gap Band. When that song came on, everyone would rush out onto the floor and skate.

There were a lot of cute and pretty girls there, but I had the best-looking one of all, and my dumb ass was still too shy to kiss her. One day I would get up the nerve; I just hoped she didn't break up with me before then.

Cindy and I talked a lot on the phone. One night, she wanted to dedicate a song to me and listen to it while she played it over the phone. It was Lionel Richie's *Hello*. And still, to this day, it remains my favorite love song of all time.

Chapter 18

Since my brother Joey and I shared a room, he would always get dressed in front of me. He wasn't near as shy as I was because he would get completely naked. I always laughed and called him "stubby," and he would call me "peach fuzz." I don't know how he knew it at the time because I would never dare get naked in front of him. But he was right; I was fourteen and didn't have any pubic hair at all.

Joey and I were both into girls, so we started hanging girl posters all over our room. The first one we got was of Farrah Fawcett in her red bathing suit, with her nipples showing through it. We also had Loni Anderson and Heather Locklear. I would go to Spencer Gifts and Kmart and buy all the girl posters I could find. Pretty soon, we had every inch of our room covered in girl posters—over one hundred of them. We had a really cool bedroom.

We were both also into music. The local pop stations were Y-106 and BJ-105; WDIZ was hard rock, Zeta-7 was classic rock, and K-92 was country. I liked all music, but my favorite was classic rock.

My mom had a bunch of old forty-five records that I would always look through. One day, I found a record in there by Ray Stevens that had a song on it called "Guitarzan." It was the funniest song I ever heard. I would play it over and over and laugh uncontrollably every time. I must have listened to that song a hundred times.

My favorite bands and singers growing up in the '80s were Kiss, Foreigner, The Eagles, Whitesnake, Quiet Riot, Phil Collins, Ozzy Osbourne, Rat, Rush, Pat Benatar, Fleetwood Mac, Bob Seger, White Lion, Def Leppard, Billy Squire, Journey, Twisted Sister, Cinderella, Charlie Daniels Band, Warrant, Pink Floyd, Herbie Hancock, Tom Petty, John Cougar Mellencamp, Led Zeppelin, Poison, Prince, Dire Straits, and Van Halen. But my favorite of all was Mötley Crüe.

I also loved comedy tapes. Richard Pryor's tape was really popular, but my mom wouldn't let my brother and me listen to it because it was too vulgar and X-rated, but we bought it anyway, and would go into our room, lock the door, and put it into our cassette deck with the volume down really low so only we could hear it. We also had Robin Williams and Eddie Murphy's tapes, which were just as bad, so we had to sneak and listen to those. But there was one comedy tape that we were allowed to listen to, and that was by Weird Al Yankovic, who was funny as hell because he would make fun of other people's songs.

Chapter 19

People need love the most
when they deserve it the least.
—Matthew 5:44

Around this time, I started getting really scared of my stepfather. I noticed he drank a lot when he came home from work, then he would get really moody, so that is when I would go outside and play or find something else to do. I didn't want to be anywhere near him when he got like that.

One time, our family stayed at a Holiday Inn, and we were all hanging out by the pool. I couldn't swim, so I always hung out in the low end. I got out of the pool to walk around, and my dad started to chase me, saying he was gonna throw me in the deep end. That just traumatized me, so I ran away from the pool and stayed away for the rest of the day.

That was just the beginning of the terror that I would receive from him. Even though he probably did it in a playful manner, there was nothing funny about what would happen later on.

My stepdad tried to be a good dad, I guess. He bought me a go-cart, took me fishing, played Frisbee with me, took me on that trip to Arcadia, took me to watch wrestling, taught me to drive, but he would never go to any of my baseball games, which I never understood.

I will never forget all the good things he did, but things started to go downhill once I started high school and got a little rebellious. But it was just typical teenage stuff.

Chapter 20

One day, I was out flying my kite, but instead of kite string, I would use fishing line, which would make the kite go so high, I could barely see it. Then Robert came over, and we went off to do our crazy shit as always.

One time, we found an old motorcycle in the woods without a motor—because people just dumped all kinds of shit in the woods back then; nobody cared about the environment. We would find all kinds of cool stuff. The motorcycle had wheels and everything else on it, so we decided to take it to the road where we used to make our roadblocks and lay it down in the middle of the street. But we would lay down on the ground with it, pretending we crashed and act like we were dead while waiting for someone to stop and help us. Then, as soon as someone stopped, we would get up and start laughing while running away. That was really funny.

On the Fourth of July, we would get a bunch of fireworks. My favorites were bottle rockets, smoke bombs, and M-80s. Robert and I would get some bottle rockets and go into the woods next to the AFCOM warehouse and shoot bottle rockets through the big rollup doors they had, which were only about fifty yards away. It was so funny because all the workers would come running outside, not knowing what was happening, while Robert and I would be hiding in the woods, laughing our asses off.

Then we would take the M-80s and blow up whatever we could find. Putting them in mailboxes was the coolest, but the funniest thing we did was with the smoke bombs.

We would look for houses that had their garage doors opened, then go in their garage and light the smoke bombs until it was smoking like hell. Then we would knock on the door that led into the house and run like hell.

I did a whole lot of running away from shit back then and would continue running from shit for my entire life.

Chapter 21

I was at my girlfriend Cindy's house one day, watching her dad wash his beautiful '67 Corvette, which was the nicest car I had ever seen. Man, I would love to have a car like that someday. Then Cindy came out and asked me if I wanted to go ride bikes, so we went riding and ended up going down Murphy Road, where there was a little bridge that crosses over a small creek that we stopped on, and that's when she told me she wanted to talk to me about something. I asked her what she wanted to talk about, and she told me she was getting ready to move to another city.

I was devastated, I couldn't believe it.

Then she asked me if I could do her a favor.

"Sure," I said.

That's when she asked if I could give her a kiss before she left. She didn't even give me time to answer. She just grabbed me and started to kiss me on the lips—tongue, and all.

It was my first and best kiss ever. I will never forget what a great feeling it was.

We must have kissed for over five minutes.

Cars drove by, honking at us, but we kept kissing. I didn't want that feeling to end. I was kissing the prettiest girl in school. Man, I felt so lucky, but I was also heartbroken at the same time. I couldn't believe she was gonna leave me and move to another town. What was I gonna do?

Chapter 22

I spent a lot of time in the woods; I loved the solitude and peacefulness. I would either be hunting with my BB gun, trying to catch snakes and turtles or just looking for wood to build my forts with. I was almost always out there by myself, finding something cool on my little journeys. Then, one day, I hit the jackpot; I found a whole garbage bag full of *Playboy* magazines. I couldn't believe my luck; there were over 100 of them.

As I was looking at them, I got the feeling I wasn't alone; I felt somebody was watching me. Sure enough, I saw a man behind a tree about fifty yards away. I knew he was waiting for me to leave, so he could get them, but I wasn't gonna let that happen. I couldn't carry them all because they were too heavy, so I carried as many as I could to a different spot, then came back and got the rest. I eventually got them all home and hid them in the woods behind my house; then, I had to wait for my mom to leave so I could sneak them all into my bedroom without her seeing me.

I couldn't wait to show my brother Joey. I also couldn't wait until I could go in my room, lock the door and look at them all, one by one. I felt like I struck gold, man; I was in heaven, and this was at the time I was really loving girls, especially after I had just kissed Cindy.

All I could think about were girls, girls, girls, especially the ones in the magazines. They were all so sexy and beautiful.

My favorite pictures were the natural blondes with blue or green eyes, with the blonde hair on their pussies. I also loved the women with tan lines from their bikinis. I loved that contrast between white and tan skin. My dick would always get so hard while looking at them, but I never knew what jacking off was or how to masturbate, so I never came. I didn't even know how or what that meant; I just knew I would always get hard and stay hard for a long time, especially when I started high school. That's when things started getting really crazy.

Chapter 23

One night I was walking by the Afcom warehouse behind my house and noticed all the office lights on in front of the building; there was also a car parked out front. It was around 8 p.m., so I decided to get nosy, wondering who could be in there so late because Afcom closed at five.

The Windows were long and narrow, about eight inches wide, four feet tall, and about three feet off the ground, so I could walk right up to them and look in with no problem. There were about twenty-five windows that ran around the whole front of the building where the offices were.

Wow! I couldn't believe what I fucking saw when I looked in one of them. There were two teenage girls in there cleaning. One was dumping trash from all the desks, and the other one was vacuuming. Oh, my fucking God, they were fine, one of them was my age, and the other one was around seventeen. They both had long black hair, tight-ass jeans, and nice fucking asses. They looked Puerto Rican and obviously sisters. I couldn't believe what was happening. My dick got hard instantly. The older one was vacuuming from one section to the next, so I just kept jumping from window to window, following her; I couldn't believe what I was seeing.

I watched them for about thirty minutes, when I saw an older lady, who was obviously their mom because she looked Puerto Rican too. Then, all three of them disappeared somewhere in the back. Then, all the lights started going off, one by one, and that's when I took off running across the street into the woods to position myself so I could see them come out of the building without them seeing me. As soon as I got in the woods, I pulled my dick out and started playing with it, waiting for them to come out.

When they came out, they put all their cleaning supplies into their car, then left. They must have been the janitors who cleaned there every night. All I could think about was, *Please, come back again.*

I then looked at my watch to make sure I would be there at exactly the same time the following night, praying they would be back.

Seeing them ignited something inside of me. I don't know if it was lust, passion, or what, but I was excited. Something about that whole experience just drove me crazy.

I went home that night feeling really good and couldn't wait until the following night. They were all I could think about. I even thought about them all day in school. All I wanted to do was get back there to see if they showed up again. Nothing else mattered.

Chapter 24

As soon as it got dark, I went over to Afcom, which was less than a five-minute walk from my house, and couldn't believe what I saw. Hell yeah, they were back. I saw their car in the parking lot and got so excited, my heart was beating really fast, my dick got instantly hard, and my adrenaline was pumping big time because I knew they would be there for at least two hours. It was only 6 o'clock.

I immediately went to the windows to see where they were and saw the big sister right away. She was vacuuming right next to the window. Goddam, she was fine. I knew she couldn't see me because it was dark outside and really bright in the offices, so I pulled down my pants and started jacking off, which was such an exhilarating experience—knowing I was so close to her, and her not knowing what I was doing. I just followed her from window to window while masturbating the whole time, which ended up becoming a nightly ritual for me. It's all I looked forward to from that night on.

As the nights went on, I started to get a little bolder; seeing them every night just got me hornier and hornier, so one night, I decided to do something a little different. I decided to take all my clothes off in the woods and leave them there, then walk up to the windows totally naked, which gave me a lot better feeling, but I would always be very cautious and make sure there weren't any other people around who could see me. But I didn't worry about that too much because the building was pretty isolated, so I felt safe walking up to the windows naked. With no clothes to hassle with, it made me even hornier. After weeks of doing that, I decided to get even bolder. I wanted to show them how big and hard they made me.

Chapter 25

Outside the front doors of Afcom was lit up pretty good, so one night, I decided to wait for all three of them to come out after they were finished cleaning, then walk up to them completely naked. Yeah, I was going to show them. It would be even more exhilarating than looking in the windows. Just the excitement leading up to that moment was overwhelming, especially when I started to see the lights going off, one by one. Knowing they were getting ready to come out was the greatest feeling ever.

When they all came out the front door, I was only ten feet away from them when they saw me. They all screamed, then ran back inside and locked the door. That's when I also took off running back to my clothes, put them on as fast as I could, then ran home before they called the police. That was my very first flashing incident, which was the greatest feeling ever.

I stayed away from Afcom for about a week after that just in case they called the cops. I didn't want them to catch me—now that would be devastating—but I did go back, and they were there as usual. The coast was also clear—no cops or other strange cars nearby. So I took all my clothes off and kept them in a neat pile in the woods, walked up to the windows, and saw them again, but this time I had a different idea.

If I stood right up to the window, they wouldn't be able to see my dick because the window was too high, so I needed something to stand on. That way, I could knock on the window, get their attention, then press my dick against the glass and show them that way. So I went to search for something to stand on and found a five-gallon bucket that was the perfect height. But I had to wait for the older sister to vacuum because she would get the closest to the window doing that, and it didn't take long before she was right there, just feet away from me on the other side of the glass. So I jumped up on the bucket, pressed my hard dick against the glass, and started knocking on the window real hard so she could hear me over the vacuum. She looked up right away, saw me, smiled, and just kept on vacuuming; then she left, probably going to tell her mom, so I took off running back to my clothes, then home. Wow! What an incredible feeling. It was so fucking fun, and I was just fourteen years old.

The following night, I wanted to get the younger sister, so I went and got my bucket and was walking up to the windows completely naked, when I saw a man walking down the street in front of Afcom. He saw me, oh my God, then he yelled, "Hey, what are you doing?"

That's when I ran like hell. I didn't know who he was, but he scared the shit out of me. So that was the last time I went there for a while. I didn't want to push my luck, but I sure did fall in love with Puerto Ricans, especially their asses.

Chapter 26

Oviedo High School was the home of the Lions. I didn't play any sports; the only sport I really liked was baseball, and I sucked at that, so I obviously wasn't good enough to play on the high school team.

I didn't hang out with anyone. I guess it was because I wasn't cool enough. So I just kept to myself and thought about girls a lot. It's funny how extremely shy I was, even though I had exposed myself to the girls at Afcom. All I could think about was what other girls I could show my dick to. I couldn't do it during school because that would be too risky.

It was just so thrilling, being completely naked and looking in the windows at Afcom. That's all I could think about, but I couldn't let anyone find out what I was doing. I didn't know what I would do if anyone ever caught me doing that.

I hated going to school. My grades weren't very good, but I loved all the pretty girls that went there, especially one girl in particular named Dee Dee, who was on the dance team. She was really short, with long brown hair, and had the nicest ass in the whole school. She would wear really tight Jordache jeans, so I would always go look for her without her seeing me, just so I could stare at her ass as much as possible. It was so nice. I was definitely too shy to talk to her, but even if I wasn't shy, she would never have given me the time of day, so all I could do was masturbate, thinking of her perfect ass. She was even sexier when she wore her little dance uniform. I must have jacked off 100 times thinking of her.

Another pretty girl who always got my dick hard was Erin, the most popular cheerleader for our football team. She had blond hair, blue eyes, and was so fucking pretty. She was also our homecoming queen. During our pep rallies on Fridays, she would do a bunch of backflips, and her little cheerleading skirt would lift up, and I could see her nice ass and her little black bikini bottom. She was the other fantasy girl I always masturbated to.

I did have a girl who liked me in school, but she wasn't as fine as Dee Dee or Erin. Her name was Luanne. I knew she liked me because every day after science class, she would make it a point to walk past me in the hallway and smile. She wasn't in any of my classes, so it became a daily ritual for us to walk by each other and smile. I know she liked me, but I was too scared to stop and talk to her, but I always looked forward to seeing her smile at me.

I remember being around other kids and hearing them tell jokes and laugh, and I would always hear them say the word "cum," and then laugh. So I always wondered why they always laughed when they said that word. I had no idea what that meant. Even though I constantly masturbated and exposed myself to girls, I had yet to experience an orgasm, so I didn't even know what that was or even felt like. I just knew my dick would always get hard when I thought about girls, so I would play with it, and that alone was a great feeling. I always wondered what cum was. We didn't have a sex-ed class, and I never was taught about sex from my parents, so I was totally clueless.

Chapter 27

One day after school, I decided to walk by Afcom when the parking lot was full of cars. It was exactly 4:45 p.m. I knew the time because I looked at my watch as soon as I saw her. Wow! She was really pretty. I saw her walking through the parking lot; she was in her 20s, wearing a short skirt and high heels. Oh my God, she was beautiful, with long brown hair. She didn't notice me, which was a good thing because I came up with a brilliant idea.

I watched her get into a brand-new blue Camaro, which made her even sexier. She must have been a secretary. I then watched her pull out of the parking lot and drive down the road, which was lined on both sides with woods. It was perfect for what I had in mind.

I walked toward the woods about thirty yards from where all the cars had to pull out of the parking lot and started looking for a good vantage point behind some trees. I needed to be able to view the whole parking lot, so I could see who was walking to their cars from the office building, but I had to make sure they couldn't see me.

As soon as I found a good spot, a mad rush of cars started to come by all at once. It was 5 o'clock, everyone was getting off work, so I hid in the woods at the spot I had found and watched every passing car to see who was driving them. I needed to remember what cars the women were driving and if they were pretty or not, but there were just too many, all coming by at once. I had to wait until it died down a little bit because I had a plan.

My plan was to take all my clothes off and masturbate while pretty women drove by me, but first, I had to find out which girls drove which cars. After that, I would have to wait until they pulled out onto the street; then they would have to be the only car coming by at that time. I couldn't risk any men driving by at the same time, coming up behind or in front of the woman. So, everything had to be timed just right. I noticed the best time was either when the women left a little bit early or late. There was no way I could do anything when all the workers left at once. Hopefully, the girl in the Camaro would leave every day, like she did that day, fifteen minutes early.

Chapter 28

What's wrong with me?
Something's broken.
                    — Richard Paul Evans

I was back in the woods next to Afcom the following day. It started becoming a daily ritual for me. I just couldn't wait to get out of school and go there. It was just so exciting, knowing I had a new plan. There was so much adrenaline pumping through me. Just thinking about it, my dick would even get hard just walking there. I had found the perfect spot.

The first thing I did when I got there was take all my clothes off. It was the first time I had taken all my clothes off during the day. It was the greatest feeling having the sun hitting my naked body. My dick was so fucking hard with the anticipation what I was gonna do; it was the greatest feeling that ever had in my life.

Just a few minutes before 5 p.m., my girl came walking out to her car alone. Yes, it was perfect. Now I knew she came out at the same time every day. I didn't do anything at first. My plan was to come out from the woods and walk out to the side of the road completely naked right as she was driving by me. But I was thinking I should at least try to disguise myself in some kind of way. The only thing I could come up with was to put my T-shirt on my head, not to cover my face, but to cover my hair, which was the only hair I had on my body. So, I would do that.

I spent every weekday at that spot just masturbating, while staring at the parking lot, seeing which cars the women got into.

After about a month of doing that, I finally knew which cars all the pretty girls were driving, and if they were by themselves or with other girls. I definitely knew which cars to stay away from; those were the ones the men drove.

I was now ready to take action. Damn, there were a lot of pretty girls, but my favorite was still the girl in the Camaro. She would be the first one I do it to. But one thing I noticed was after jacking off every day for over a month, my dick was getting sore in a certain spot. That really started to bother me, so when I got home, I went into the bathroom and found some lotion that I could take with me the following day, which would sure make a huge difference.

It felt so much better to masturbate with lotion. I couldn't believe I went so long without using it, so I ended up bringing it with me every day.

My mom and sisters would always want to know where their lotion went; now they know it was me stealing it.

Chapter 29

I finally decided it was time to show the girl in the Camaro how hard she made me.

I watched her and every other girl who worked there for months. It was time to show them all, one by one, but I was gonna start with Camaro girl. I knew it would probably take a while because, in every case, the situation had to be just right. Like I said earlier, they would have to drive by themselves with no men in front or behind them. But if two cars came at once and I knew both of them had women in them, then I would get both at once.

On that day, I got out there at 4 p.m. and took all my clothes off. I just loved the feeling of being naked outside in the sun. I put lotion all over my dick and started jacking off, thinking about the girl in the Camaro, hoping and praying that she would drive by. The anticipation was unbelievable. There was no other feeling like it. Then, before I knew it, I saw her in a red dress walking to her car by herself. *Hell, yes, please, no men coming out behind her, please, please, please.*

So far, so good, it was really gonna happen. I couldn't believe it. She got into her car, backed out of the parking space, and was driving toward the exit—still by herself, without another car in sight. Fuck yeah. *Are you ready, baby? Are you ready for a real shocking surprise?*

My T-shirt was on my head. I had my sneakers on to avoid stepping on anything sharp. My dick was all lotioned up and hard as a rock. Nothing was stopping me. As soon as I saw her car pull out onto the street, I ran out to the side of the road and started waving my dick at her from side to side. She saw me and just shook her head and kept driving. *How did you like that?*

I then ran back into the woods and put my clothes on really fast. I needed to get out of there before she told somebody.

Yes, I finally got to show her. Hell yeah. What a rush that was. Man, I couldn't wait to go back the following day and do it to another girl. Or maybe I would get Camaro girl again. Wow! What a day, that was fun. I couldn't believe I was only fourteen years old and exposing myself to women. I wondered what they thought when they saw me. Did they know how young I was?

Chapter 30

I went out to my spot, just like I did every day for months. I knew I was pushing my luck. I pretty much exposed myself to every girl at Afcom who I thought was hot, but I just couldn't stop. I loved the feeling of being naked in the woods, jacking off, exposing myself to women. It was the greatest feeling ever.

At around 4:30, I saw two Camaros drive by. I didn't think too much about them, except that they were the exact same year as Camaro Girl's, just different colors. I let that thought pass and continued to jack off while watching the parking lot. Then, right before 5 o'clock, Camaro Girl came walking out, looking sexier than ever in a short yellow miniskirt and high heels. *Dam, I might as well get her again.* I put my T-shirt on my head, put more lotion on my already rock-hard dick, and got ready to run out there.

Then all hell broke loose.

I couldn't believe what was happening. The two Camaros I saw earlier were racing toward me at a high rate of speed. *Oh shit.* They were after me. I heard brakes screeching, doors slamming, and guys screaming, "get him." There were two guys from both cars who were bound and determined to do whatever they could to catch me. I barely had enough time to grab my pants, let alone put them on, but I knew I had to grab them because I would be horrified to get away and then be without clothes. How would I ever get back home and into my house naked?

I took off running as fast as I could. I had never been so scared in my life. They were very close to me. All I could think of was, *Please, God, don't let them catch me.* I knew they would beat me up, and no telling what else. They were grown men in their 20s and were in good shape because they were keeping up with me, and I was really fast. I was running around trees like a jackrabbit, running for my life, completely naked. There was no way in hell I could let them catch me. They chased me through the woods for what seemed like forever, when all of a sudden, I couldn't believe it; I looked back and saw that they had finally given up.

I ended up staying in the woods until it got dark. Then I finally got brave enough to walk home. Needless to say, I never went to that spot ever again. I needed to take a break after that. It was a very traumatizing experience for me. It was my worst fear coming true. I couldn't even imagine getting caught for something like that.

Nobody in my family or any of my friends had a clue what I did, and I wanted to keep it that way. So, I took some time off until I could come up with some other way to flash women.

Chapter 31

Around 1984, my mom bought the drive-through store where she worked, which was really cool. I know my mom was proud of that, and we were all happy for her. She also changed the name to Rosemary's Beverage Barn, which was also a gas station. All of us kids would go there and help her out. She taught us the prices of everything—how to use the register and stock the shelves. There were no barcodes to scan back then, so the hard part was remembering what everything cost. But what I enjoyed the most about working there were all the pretty girls that came through. They would drive up, and I would walk up to their car and hand them whatever they wanted, which was mostly milk, bread, beer, sodas, and small stuff like that. I would look down, and there would be some women with their dresses and miniskirts hiked so far up, I could see their panties. I think they did that on purpose. I saw some really nice legs too.

But there was one thing I was really scared of. My mom's store was located on Highway 434 in Winter Springs, on the corner of Belle Avenue, which was the street Afcom was on. Which scared the shit out of me. The companies down that street were my mom's main customers. Can you see why I was scared? I only flashed about every woman that worked at Afcom. That's what terrified me. I disguised myself with a T-shirt on my head, but would that be enough for them not to recognize me. I was fully clothed at the store, so hopefully, that helped.

But I was still paranoid as hell working there. I wasn't as scared on the weekends because Afcom was closed. I was also scared to death of Camaros, especially blue ones.

Thank God I was never recognized working there. I know that would've really embarrassed my mom, along with traumatizing me. I couldn't even imagine getting caught for what I was doing. I knew it wasn't normal behavior. But I loved working there.

One summer, a Camaro came through the store. It seemed like all the hot chicks drove Camaros back then. It was a very popular car, or maybe I was just noticing them more, but anyway, this really hot chick pulled up in a maroon one wearing a bikini. She was around nineteen. I recognized the car because she lived on Cortez Avenue, only a couple blocks away from my house, but I never met or talked to her. Damn, she was hot. The thing that turned me on the most was that she was really tan and had this blonde peach fuzz on her stomach. To see her in a bikini drove me crazy. After seeing her come through the store that day, I would always walk by her house just to see if she would be outside so I could see her again.

There was one girl in particular who came to the store that I was really in love with. Not only did she have a fucking badass car, but she was the prettiest girl I had ever seen up until that point. She had naturally blonde hair and green eyes, which I loved, and a bright green two-seater, 69 AMX., with chrome Cragar mag wheels, a 390 engine, and a four-speed manual transmission. Not only was I in love with her, I was in love with her car.

I did my best and tried to talk to her a little every time she came by, and I think she started to like me because she started coming by more and more. Then one day, I finally got the nerve to ask her where she lived, which wasn't far from my house, so I asked if she would like to come over sometime. I knew she would never give me the time of day, but I asked her anyway.

She was older than me, had a job, her own car, was fucking fine, and could have any guy she wanted. I was just a skinny fifteen-year-old with no job or car. She wouldn't even think about going out with me. So, I was in shock when she actually came over to my house one night. I couldn't believe it—a hot chick with a car was over my house talking to me in my driveway. Wow! I was in heaven. Then, BAM, after about an hour of us talking, she hit me with I'm too young, and she was probably too old for me. Which was true. She could have got in trouble for messing around with me, but I damn sure wasn't gonna tell anyone. I was still a virgin; I just wanted to kiss her and be her boyfriend.

Damn, I fantasized about her so much after that night. I even went so far as to walk by her house, trying to look in her bedroom window at night to see if I could catch her undressing. I never got that chance because her curtains were always closed, but I always thought about her when I jacked off. I wish I could've shown her how big and hard she made me. She even stopped coming by the store after that night, so I was heartbroken. At least she got me loving '69 AMXs.

Chapter 32

I could never spend the night at my friends' houses because I had a huge problem that I was really embarrassed about. I was still wetting the bed at fifteen and would continue until I was seventeen, so I would be terrified to sleep over at anyone's house.

I went camping one time with someone from my baseball team, and I was so scared of peeing the bed, I laid awake all night just to make sure I didn't.

Darren and I would go to the driving range at Big Cypress to hit balls and practice our putting. Then, when we could afford it, we would play nine for eighteen holes. He would always beat me because I sucked at golf.

One day, after we were finished hitting balls, I was walking toward the clubhouse, when an old man in his sixties drove up to me in a golf cart and asked if I needed a job. Darren was using the bathroom at the time. I told the old man that I was only fifteen, and he said that was OK. He said it was really easy work, that all I had to do was wash golf carts. Then he told me to come back the following day when the manager would be there, so he could introduce me to him. I said OK, then left. I went to tell Darren what had happened. Wow! It sounded like a pretty cool job to have, so I went home that night all excited and told my mom, who thought it was great and was happy for me.

I went back the next day and talked to the manager, who hired me on the spot and told me to go out and see the old man, who would show me what to do. He even gave me my own timecards that I had to fill out every day. It was a really fun job. All I had to do was wash the carts when they came in, then drive them into a big building and plug them in so they could charge overnight. I had to stay until the last cart came in, then I would have to lock them up before I could leave.

The old man was really nice to me. I was there for a couple of weeks before he trusted me enough to lock up all the carts by myself. The clubhouse closed at 5 p.m., but I would have to stay later, waiting for all the carts to come in, usually around six or seven, sometimes later.

I don't know what made me do it, but this was the first time I began to cheat and lie. I would have to turn in my timecard every Friday, and I was always the last one to leave, so nobody knew when I left. I started writing down that I left at 8 p.m. every night, which wasn't true because most of the time, I would be done by six. By doing that, I would get paid for about ten extra hours per week. I never got caught.

While I was working, I would constantly be thinking of how exciting it was when I was exposing myself to the women at Afcom, and I wanted to do it again, but it was just too risky. I needed to find another way because all I wanted to do was be naked in the woods masturbating.

Chapter 33

One Saturday, I grabbed one of my Playboys out of my closet and some lotion, then went and found a nice, secluded spot in the woods on the edge of the sand dunes and took all my clothes off. I just loved the feeling of the sun beating down on my naked body while I masturbated. I looked at my magazine and masturbated for eight hours straight. It was the greatest feeling in the world. I didn't want to be doing anything else.

I ended up doing that every weekend. Sometimes I would hide my clothes and just see how far I could walk through the woods and dunes completely naked without anyone seeing me.

After months of doing that, I was constantly thinking of how I could expose myself to more women without getting caught. I would have my answer soon enough.

Chapter 34

One day when I went to work, I was talking to the old man, and he was telling me that I could make extra money selling golf balls. I asked him what he was talking about, and he said that he goes into the woods along the fairways and looks for balls. He said that he had found thousands of them, which he then sold to golfers for $0.25 and $0.50, depending on their condition.

Wow! That sounded like a good idea to me.

Then he asked if I wanted to go look for them with him.

"Sure."

So, we went out into the woods and were out there for about ten minutes when he said he had to pee. He said he liked to pee out there because it was a lot closer than walking all the way to the clubhouse. So, he started taking a piss, and instead of facing with his back to me, he faced sideways so I could see his penis. He wasn't even peeing, as far as I could tell. He was just shaking and playing with it until I looked, which I thought was really weird. He then pretended to finish, and we continued to look for balls. He would do that every time we looked for balls.

While he was always pretending to be peeing, he would always ask me, "You sure you don't have to pee?"

"No, I'm OK. I don't have to go."

But he would always make sure I saw his dick.

I never did tell my boss; I just stopped going in the woods with him. He was making me feel really uncomfortable. I could look for balls without him.

I also got to work on the driving range, picking up all the balls, which was really fun because I got to drive a machine with a cage around it so I wouldn't get hit by balls. It was fun because all the golfers would try to hit me. I also had to pick up carts that were broken down on the golf course, mainly because their batteries would die.

What I enjoyed the most was all the stuff I would find left behind in the golf carts. I would find loose change, balls, wallets, clubs, but the best thing I would find was beer, especially on the weekends. The carts would come back full of beer that the golfers wouldn't finish, so I would take them home and hide them in the woods behind my house, then Robert and I would drink them.

When I was at work, I would hunt for balls every chance I got. The golfers would buy them from me really fast, which was easy money. I even went into all the lakes and ponds on my days off, looking for them. One day I was in the woods behind one of the greens; it might have been the fifth hole. The golfers would tee off, then there was a dried-up creek bed that they had to clear on their second shot to reach the green, which was the most secluded one on the course. It was surrounded by woods. To get to the next tee, you had to take a trail through the woods and over a small bridge. As I was looking for balls around that green, I saw a really old lady all by herself teeing off.

That's what triggered an idea.

I could expose myself to golfers as they were getting ready to hit their balls over the creek toward the green. Or

I could just wait for them to putt, then expose myself to them at that time. The setting was perfect; the woods were the perfect cover for me. I could hide in them and still see all the golfers approaching the green. I could even see as far as the tee, so I would know who was coming in advance.

Hell yeah, it was perfect. I now had a plan for my next day off, and I couldn't fucking wait.

Chapter 35

I got up real early on Saturday morning and told my mom I was going to look for golf balls on the golf course to sell. I then grabbed my bottle of lotion, got on my bike, and headed over there. I rode to Sheoah Boulevard, which was the street that ran through the community that the golf course also ran through. About a mile down Sheoah, by the tennis courts, was a bike path that ran through the woods, which I loved to ride my bike on. I took that path because I knew it went through the woods that were closest to the green where I wanted to go. When I reached that spot, I got off my bike, made sure nobody was coming up or down the path, then ducked into the woods. Once I was in there, I found a good place to hide my bike, then went to look for a good vantage point where I could hide but still be able to see all the golfers that came onto the green, and also the ones that were teeing off.

Once I found that spot, I took off all my clothes. Man, what a great feeling. I loved the warm sun hitting my body and the smell of the fresh-cut grass. My dick got hard as always, so I put lotion on and started masturbating. I could stay out there all day, which I did.

I wasn't too concerned about flashing anyone at first. I just wanted to be naked in the woods, jacking off. Plus, there were too many men on the course—just a steady stream of them, group after group. Also, a lot of maintenance guys would come by, so I had to be careful and always hide from them.

When there were no golfers around, I walked out onto the green by the flag, just to see how it felt, and pretended I was flashing the golfers. As I was doing that, I saw an old lady getting ready to tee off, so I ran back into the woods so she wouldn't see me. My heart was beating so fast because she was all by herself. She had to be in her 70s, but I didn't care because I was so horny, I decided I was going to flash her just for the hell of it. I then put more lotion on and started masturbating like crazy. I would wait for her to get onto the green and finish putting, then I would come out of the woods and just walk up to her completely naked.

So that's what I did. I walked right up to her as she was putting her putter back in her bag, and she completely ignored me. She didn't even say anything and walked away to the next tee. It had me wondering if she even saw me. But she had to. I was standing ten feet from her. I then ran back into the woods before any other golfers came.

I stayed in those woods for ten hours until it got dark and couldn't wait to do it all again the following day.

Chapter 36

I was back at the golf course bright and early Sunday morning to do it all again. There was a steady stream of men as usual, but no old ladies. I was there again for about ten hours and was about to leave when I saw four guys getting ready to tee off. They had to be the last group coming through, so I decided, *what the hell*, it was my last day there until the following weekend, so I might as well do something I've never done.

I was gonna flash some men. That would be funny. So I waited until they were all on the other side of the dried-up creek bed about 100 yards away, which would give me plenty of time to flash them, run back into the woods, put my clothes on, get on my bike, and get the hell out of there. So that's what I did. I waited until they were all hitting their balls towards the green, then ran out onto the green and started waving my dick at them.

When they saw me, I heard one of the guys yell to his friend, "Hey, look, there's a naked guy on the green."

Then they all started yelling. I noticed one of their balls was one of those cool, green, fluorescent ones, so I grabbed it, then hauled ass away from there as fast as I could. My adrenaline was really pumping as I rode away on my bike. Man, that was a fun day. I couldn't wait to do it again.

I was so excited that I had found a new spot to mastur-bate and flash. I wasn't too thrilled about flashing old ladies or men, but that was all about to change very soon.

Chapter 37

A few weeks later, while I was at work washing carts, I looked toward the clubhouse and couldn't believe my eyes. There were girls everywhere—not old ladies either. These were fine-ass girls, in their late teens, early twenties—about twenty of them in all, and they were all carrying golf bags, getting ready to play the course. A group of them were walking toward the first tee. I couldn't believe it.

Right then and there, I knew what I was gonna do. I noticed all their golf bags said "Rollins College" on them. They were from that college in Winter Park and were members of their golf team.

Oh my God. Hell yeah.

I made sure none of the girls or my boss saw me get onto my bike and sneak out of there. I rode through the parking lot, onto Highway 434, to Sheoah Boulevard. as fast as I could, then I took that to the bike trail. I knew I had plenty of time because the girls were just teeing off at the first hole. So, it would be a while before they reached the fifth.

My heart was racing with excitement when I got into the woods by the fifth green. I hid my bike, got to my favorite vantage point, took off all my clothes, then waited. Man, I was so excited because I knew what was coming. No longer men, after men, after men, and the occasional old lady.

There was gonna be fine girl, after fine girl, after fine girl, coming right to me. Wow!

I was there for less than an hour when I saw the first group of them approaching the tee. There were four girls in each group, and I would be able to choose any group I wanted. There would be at least five of them. I could just flash them all. I didn't know what to do. I thought it would be safer to flash just one group because I would need to get the hell out of there in case they told someone. I couldn't afford to get caught. That would be devastating, I had to play it safe, so I would just flash the first group, plus I didn't want to be away from work that long, I was already gone long enough as it was.

Oh fuck. They were right on the other side of the creek, hitting their balls toward the green. I would wait for them to finish putting, then step out of the woods and flash all four of them when they were all together. Wow! They were all pretty. I couldn't believe what was happening.

Chapter 38

I stepped out of the woods, and they saw me right away. I was about twenty yards away from them when I froze in my tracks. They all looked at me and asked what I was doing. I was afraid to go any closer, so I just started masturbating while looking at them.

A lot was going through my mind. The first thing I thought was how pretty, cute, and fine they all were. *Oh my God.* Then I thought they could all grab me if I got any closer, or they could hit me with their golf clubs. I was like a deer frozen in headlights.

But what amazed me the most was they were not moving. They were all just watching me jack off.

Then one of them said, "come here," and that's when I started to feel something. It was hard to describe because I had never felt anything like it before, but it felt like something was happening with my penis, and it felt really good. It felt so good that I couldn't stop jacking off. The more I jacked off, the better it was feeling. I didn't have any idea what was happening, but I couldn't stop, and the girls kept on watching me when all of a sudden, all this white stuff started shooting out of my dick. It just kept shooting out and shooting out.

Oh my God. What was going on?

And that's when it hit me. It must be what cum was, which everybody in school was talking about.

After I came all over the golf course in front of them, I took off back into the woods, and the girls said, "Where are you going?"

I got dressed as fast as I could, got on my bike, and went back to work, hoping they wouldn't tell anyone.

Wow! That was the most exhilarating thing I have ever experienced in my life. It was also the first time I ever came, so from that moment on, I loved college girls and wanted to find more of them—and I would find more, thousands more. They also became my favorite girls to flash. I loved them.

When I got back to work, I was paranoid. Thank God my boss didn't even know I left. What I was most afraid of was when the girls finished golfing, I couldn't let them see me. They might recognize me because, in all my excitement, I forgot to put my T-shirt on my head, and they knew exactly what I looked like, which was not good.

I was so scared and paranoid for the rest of that afternoon and evening.

I saw them come in and leave without anything happening—no police, no boss calling me into his office. They didn't tell anyone, which made me feel a lot better. But my luck was about to change, and my days at the golf course were numbered.

Chapter 39

I was at work Monday when the old man came up to me and said the boss was in his office and wanted to see me.

His office door was open, and he was sitting at his desk, so I walked up to the open doorway and said, "Hey, what's up?"

The words that came out of his mouth almost gave me a heart attack. All he said to me, was "try and keep your clothes on."

I know my face turned red or white, I'm not sure which, but I knew he saw instant fear in me. I didn't know what to say. All I could utter was "OK," and I got the hell out of there as fast as I could. It was the most embarrassed I had been in my life. I couldn't even deny it because I knew my face gave me away. He never said I was fired for anything, but I knew I was quitting right then and there. I'd been caught, or at least found out. I couldn't work there anymore. There was no way. I wouldn't even be able to flash there anymore because if I did, and someone reported it to the clubhouse or police, they would know exactly who it was and come right to me.

Fuck. I would have to find another spot.

But the one thing that terrified me the most was my boss knew my mom because she owned the store right across the street. He and the other golf pros went there all the time.

I was so scared he was gonna tell my mom; I just knew he would.

I'm not sure if he ever told my mom, but if he did, she never did say anything to me about it. My boss never called the police on me either. That was a very close call. Now I was out of a job, but that was OK. I didn't like working anyway because it was taking a lot of my time away from flashing and being naked in the woods jacking off, which was a lot more exciting than washing golf carts.

That's all I thought about constantly, and it's all I wanted to do. I didn't even want to go to school anymore because when I was in school, I couldn't wait to get home, so I could go in the woods, masturbate, and look for new spots to expose myself.

It really started to take over my life. It was more impor-tant than school or work. Nothing else mattered, and now that I knew how to cum, it was even more intense and thrilling. Even after all the exposing I'd done up until that point, I was still a virgin, but I was gonna try and change that. I wanted to see what it would feel like to have sex with a girl.

Cindy was no longer around; we broke up when she moved away. I sure would've loved to have sex with her. She probably would have let me if I hadn't been so damn shy.

I would find someone; there are some girls in school that liked me.

Chapter 40

I called Robert and told him that I put the new motor on my go-kart, then asked him if he wanted to see it. So, I rode it over to his house, which was about two miles away on Murphy Road. When I got there, he was working on his minibike, so we were just hanging out when he asked me if I wanted to go to some girls' house—actually, they were two sisters. He said he knew them and that they both had big tits, and they were around our age.

"Hell yeah, let's go."

So, he finished fixing his minibike, and we took off to their house, which was also off Murphy Road. He rode his minibike, and I rode my go-kart.

Their names were Brenda and Linda. I was instantly attracted to Brenda. She was very cute, really short, and had really nice tits, especially for a fifteen-year-old girl. Man, it was love at first sight for me. Robert liked Linda, who had big-ass tits too. *Wow!*

We stayed over there for a long time, talking to them. I ended up getting Brenda's number. She liked me and wanted to know if I would be her boyfriend.

"Hell yeah, I'll be your boyfriend."

I knew right then and there that she would be the first girl I had sex with because Robert told me that she had sex with someone before.

Her parents didn't like Robert, so the only time we could go over there was when they were at work. Robert and I both had long hair at that time, so we looked like trouble, but we weren't that bad; we just liked to drink. Robert also liked to smoke. I hated smoking.

We would always ride our minibikes and go-karts by their house when their mom and dad were home, and they were really loud, so Brenda's parents really hated us for that.

Then one day, Brenda told me that her mom didn't want me around, either.

"Why? What did I do?"

She just said her mom didn't want Robert or me around their house. I never even met or talked to her mom, and she didn't even like me, so that's how our relationship went. We had to keep it hidden from her parents. But that was OK. We would make it work.

Chapter 41

Brenda and I were in love with each other, but it sucked because we had to keep our relationship secret from her parents. My mom was cool and didn't mind. We wrote a lot of letters to each other and talked on the phone every day. I saved all the letters she wrote me and kept them in my little safe that my mom bought me in Vegas. I had that thing stuffed full of letters.

Brenda also liked to drink, so we would sneak off and look for places to drink. I would only go near her house when her mom and dad were at work, so we spent most of the time hanging out at my house, in my room, talking and listening to music, but my mom wouldn't let us lock the door when we were in there together. I was still a virgin, so my mom didn't have anything to worry about. We would just kiss, but that was all about to change.

Chapter 42

Brenda asked me if I wanted to sneak over to her house around midnight and climb through her bedroom window after her parents went to sleep. "Hell yeah, I will be there."

I knew I was getting ready to have sex for the first time, so I was very nervous and excited. I couldn't wait. Just being able to lay in bed with her would be fun—let alone be naked with her under the covers. I couldn't wait to see her big tits and the rest of her body.

I was at her house, exactly at midnight, tapping on her window, and she was right there to let me in. We didn't waste any time either. We lay on her bed and started kissing. That's when she asked if I would have sex with her.

"Yeah, but it's my first time," I said. "We then got completely naked; I left my socks on, though.

She laid down on her back, and I got on top of her and started kissing her again. That's when she reached down and grabbed my dick, and helped me put it inside of her. Damn, she was nice and wet. It took me a few seconds to figure it out, but once I got the hang of it, it was on. There was no stopping me. I was going in and out of her really slow at first. Then she started moaning, telling me how good it felt, so the more she moaned, the faster I would go, and that's when I started to feel myself getting ready to cum.

Wow! What a great feeling. I will never forget that first time. After I came, I pulled out, and we just laid in bed and held each other, kissed, and talked until 3 a.m. That's when I told her I needed to leave before it got light outside. I didn't want to get caught and get into trouble.

It went really well for being my first time, and from that moment on, Brenda and I were inseparable. Plus, I was hooked on pussy.

We took turns after that. She would sneak over my house and climb through my window, then I would sneak over and climb through hers. We never did get caught.

I sure loved having sex with her. It was fun. She had a sexy little body, but even as much as I loved having sex with her, I would still get the urge to expose myself to girls. That desire was always there; it wouldn't go away. It was so strong that one day I decided I had to find a new spot to expose myself.

Chapter 43

I sure wished I had a car. I wanted to get out and explore more places. I've been to every place within walking distance of my house, but I needed to find a place that was wooded, so I could get completely naked without anyone seeing me. But, at the same time, women or girls had to come by there. That's the kind of spot I needed to find.

One day, I acted like I was sick again so I could stay home, but instead of watching music videos, I would just roam around the woods and sand dunes around my house, hoping I would get lucky and see a girl out there. I would spend the day doing that. I just pretended I was going to school; then, as I was walking to the bus stop, I would just cut in between two houses that led to the woods, then I would have to wait in the woods until the rest of my brothers and sisters left for school. I also had to wait for my mom to go to work, then I would go into the house and get my lotion and a *Playboy*, then I went to find a good spot where I could hide but also be able to see anybody out there walking by.

It didn't take long. As soon as I took all my clothes off and had my magazine spread out on the ground, I looked up and couldn't believe my eyes. There were two girls walking through the dunes about 200 yards away. They looked to be just a couple of years younger than me. Maybe around thirteen. There was no way I could flash them because I was in the woods that bordered the dunes, and the dunes were really big and open. I couldn't just run out there naked; it was just too risky.

Fuck. I didn't know what to do. They were both wearing backpacks, so they were obviously going to school, but there wasn't a school anywhere near there. I wondered where they were going. Then I got my answer when I saw them hiding their backpacks in some bushes. They were skipping school too. *Hell yeah.* I watched them hide their backpacks and waited for them to leave. That's when I came up with a plan.

I got dressed, then walked over to where they put their backpacks and thought they had to come back to get them. They didn't get away after all. I would get them when they got back, but first, I looked through their backpacks to see if there was anything good in them. They just had notepads, books, pens, and pencils—nothing worth taking, so I put them back in the bushes and found a decent spot close by where I could wait. I was really excited because I knew they had to come back. I just didn't know when, but it didn't matter. I wasn't going anywhere. I had a surprise for them. *Wow!* I picked the perfect day to go out there. My adrenaline was pumping big time; it was the greatest feeling ever.

I took all my clothes off, hid behind some bushes, and jacked off while I waited. It was around 8 a.m., so I figured they would be back around the time school let out, around 3 p.m. It didn't matter to me. I could wait all day because I knew they had to come back.

I stayed there masturbating until 3 p.m., and there was still no sign of them. I would keep waiting until it got dark.

I didn't care. I was going to make sure they saw my dick. Then 4 p.m. came, then 5 p.m. *Dammit,* where the hell were they? Then it started getting dark, and that's when I said, *fuck it.* They got lucky; I went home.

That should give you an example of how addicting my urges were becoming. I could sit in one spot for ten hours just to expose myself one time. The anticipation was amazing. I could do that all day, every day. I didn't want to be doing anything else.

Chapter 44

I started really getting scared of my stepdad when I turned sixteen, which was also the first time he ever hit me. Because I got caught skipping school, he hit me with his belt, and it really hurt. So from that moment on, I would be scared of him because he would always be drinking when he hit me, which made it even scarier.

Between all of us kids, we were always getting into some kind of trouble. My mom would also hit us with whatever she could find. She started hitting me with a wooden spoon until I hid that from her. Then she started using a vacuum cleaner belt, which I also hid. It was kinda funny because she would chase me all the way to my room until I couldn't run any further, then corner me, then start hitting me. Hers didn't hurt as much as my dad's because I could block most of them. One time she even went out into the backyard and cut some palm tree branches off a tree to hit me with because I would hide all her other stuff. It was a lot worse when my dad hit me because he was really trying to hurt me. Just the look in his icy blue eyes scared the hell outta me. I also knew he didn't love me because I wasn't his real son. I could tell because he spent more time with Bobby and never hit him.

It got to the point I didn't even want to be at home when he was there, so I would either lock myself in my room and listen to music, or I would just leave the house when he was home.

Then, when I had access to a car, things really started to go downhill.

Another thing I noticed was that my dad favored my older brother Joey a lot more than he did me because they would always go shoot pool together and never invite me.

My mom must have gotten tired of chasing me around the house trying to hit me with stuff because she just started calling my dad at work when I did something wrong, then hand the phone to me. Then my dad would tell me to "stand by" when he got home. Those were his favorite words to use. "Stand by." He was the reason I started running away from home in the first place.

I would get so scared that I would go around the house looking for all the spare change I could find. I would even go into my mom's purse and grab a couple of dollars. I needed money because as soon as my dad got home, I was gonna run away. I would stand by the front kitchen window waiting for him to pull up, then as soon as I saw his car, I would say to my mom, "I'm outta here, I'm running away." Then I would go out the back door and through the woods. I would be gone for a couple of days before I would run out of money and start getting hungry, then I would come back home.

I felt really bad because one time, I stole my mom's silver dollar collection just so I would have money when I ran away. My mom also had one of those big water cooler jugs that she kept pennies in. I could never steal the whole jug because it was too heavy, but I would always take as many pennies as I could carry.

When I ran away, I would go to the Mosswood apartments because they had motor homes and boats parked there that I could break into and sleep in. I would also sneak over to Brenda's at night and stay with her, then I would go back home and get into more trouble.

One time, I ran away and was hanging out at the sand dunes watching all the dirt bikes, quads, and big 4x4 trucks. There were some nice trucks that went there, especially the Toyotas, which were popular. I saw a nice one parked off to the side that two guys in their twenties were sitting in drinking beer. So I walked up to tell them that their truck was really nice and that I sure would love to have one like it someday. They were really cool and asked if I wanted to drink with them. That sounded good. It's not like I had anything better to do, so I hung out with them and drank all day.

I had six beers and was getting pretty drunk when they said, "Let's see what this truck can do."

It was dark by that time, so they turned on their spotlights, and I jumped in the truck with them. It was really fun. We were hauling ass through the dunes, jumping over all kinds of hills and jumps, listening to heavy metal, when I started to get really dizzy, and before I could even let them know I was getting sick, I threw up all over the floorboard. The guy next to me saw what I was doing a said to the driver, "Hey, this kid just threw up all inside your truck."

I told them that I was sorry and didn't mean to. Then the driver slammed on the brakes and told me to get the fuck out of his truck. So, I got out while still apologizing, and that's when the driver got out and punched me in the face. Then the other driver started punching me also. I fell to the ground, and the last thing I remembered was them both kicking me in the head. They must have knocked me out because all I remember was waking up the next morning with my face in the dirt and dried-up blood all over me.

I was so scared. They could have run me over and killed me if they wanted to, and nobody would've known who they were. I was unconscious in the middle of the sand dunes for at least five hours. That really scared me. I was dirty and hungry and just wanted to take a hot shower and sleep in my own bed. So, I went home and tried to avoid my dad as much as possible.

Chapter 45

I took a break from running around naked, masturbating, because I had just turned sixteen and wanted to find a job so I could buy my own car. Then the possibilities of where I could go would be endless. I also asked my mom if I could use her Datsun station wagon when I got my license since she wasn't using it anymore, and she said, "We'll see. It depends on how you behave." So, from that point on, I tried to behave myself as best I could. Then, as soon as I got my license, I asked her if I could use it to look for a job, and she let me.

The first place I went to fill out an application was a store called TG&Y. It was similar to Kmart, and they hired me. That was my first real official job. I was so excited and couldn't wait to tell my mom.

My job was to put price tags on everything and to stock the shelves. Since there were no barcodes to scan, whatever it said on that little price tag sticker was what it cost, then they manually punched that into the cash register. I was given a price tag gun and told how much things were. I also got to wear a red TG&Y vest. I was proud and happy to be working there and looked forward to going to work every day after school.

Chapter 46

Somehow, I began talking to Robert again. I'm pretty sure it was because he found out I had access to a car. He also asked if I had broken his windows at his house. He said his dad thought it was me and wanted to know why I would do that. I told him I didn't know what he was talking about. Then I told him about my new job and asked if he wanted to stop by that night while I was at work. So, he came by and found me in the automotive section, stocking shelves and putting prices on things. He came up with a brilliant idea, asking me if I could put whatever prices I wanted on stuff.

"Yes," I said. He then went looking for something that he wanted and asked if I would make it a lot cheaper so he could come back later and buy it.

"OK, just let me know how much to make it. I'll do that for you."

I don't remember what he picked out, but I do remember making it less than half price,

Then I walked with him as he was leaving.

At the front of the store, Robert stopped and talked to one of the cashiers that he knew.

Oh, my fucking God.

I froze in my tracks.

It was the first time I saw her working there. She must have been new. She was the older Puerto Rican sister from Afcom, the one I flashed and jacked off to a hundred times. I was so scared she would recognize me, so I tried to hurry Robert up.

Wow! She was even prettier up close. Thank God she didn't recognize or have a clue as to who I was. I guess I looked a lot different with clothes on.

Robert finally left and gave me that idea to look for stuff I wanted, then lower the price and come back and buy it myself.

Since my mom was letting me use the car, I might as well fix it up and pretend it was mine and buy cool stuff for it. The first thing I bought was a square, black-and-white Playboy air freshener to hang on the rearview mirror. Then I bought a set of fog lights to put on the front bumper. I tried to make the car look as cool as possible. The fog lights were $50, and I lowered them all the way down to $9.99.

Chapter 47

My job at TG&Y only lasted a couple of months. I can't remember if I got fired or quit. I had a little money saved up, so I was in no hurry to find another job. I also got to take the car to school, which was really nice because now I didn't have to act like I was sick to stay home. I would just act like I was going to school, then once I got there, I would go to homeroom or my first class, then leave. I would get Brenda, Robert, and a couple of girls Robert knew, then we would all take off back to my house. But first, I would have to park at Afcom, then walk through the woods and peek over my fence to make sure my mom, brothers, and sisters were all gone. Then I would go back to the car and tell everyone the coast was clear. I would leave the car there, and we would all go hang out in my room drinking wine coolers and listening to music until 2 p.m. Then we would take off back to school and pretend we were getting out along with everyone else. That ended up becoming a daily ritual, so I knew my days at Oviedo High were numbered.

It was especially fun when just me and Brenda would skip because we would go back to my house and fuck all day.

Chapter 48

Even though I was having sex with Brenda, which was great, it just wasn't the same feeling as exposing myself, along with the anticipation leading up to it. So, when I wasn't with her, I would be out looking for new places to flash and masturbate.

My dad was also getting more violent toward me. I'm not sure what I did wrong—I might have been caught skipping school again—but one night, we got into a shouting match, then he chased me to my room and tackled me on my bed while hitting me, telling me I had just lost the car. Then he took my keys. At that moment, I knew I couldn't live in the same house with him. He terrified me. So I came up with a plan.

My dad thought he was slick by taking my keys, but little did he know that I had made an extra one, just for that reason.

I called Brenda and told her what had happened. She was also having problems with her parents, so we decided to run away together that night.

I waited until midnight before I made my move, going out to my car and pushing it to the street so my dad wouldn't hear it start. Then I went to pick up Brenda, who was waiting for me on the corner by her house under the streetlight.

We drove to the Mosswood apartments and broke into the motor home that was parked there. All I needed was a screwdriver to pop the door open. We stayed in there and had sex until later that morning, then spent the following day driving around, trying to figure out where to go and what to do. We decided to go to the skating rink that night and do some speed and drink some wine coolers since it was a Saturday and we had nothing else to do.

Brenda and I were at the skating rink, having a good time, when I looked toward the front door and couldn't believe what I saw. It was my mom and my brother Joey. *Oh my God.* My mom was wearing a bathrobe and had curlers in her hair.

"We have to get outta here," I told Brenda.

Right at that moment, my mom saw us, started screaming at me, then started to chase us through the skating rink. How embarrassing.

Brenda and I took off through the side fire exit doors, which set off the fire alarm, then ran toward the car, where my brother was waiting for us with the key he got from my dad.

He caught us, then my mom got to the car and yelled at Brenda and me. We were so scared. I was especially scared of what my dad was gonna do to me, and Brenda was scared of what her parents were gonna do to her.

My brother drove us home while my mom followed in her Camaro. We dropped Brenda off at her house, then went home where I would get beaten again by my dad.

This time I was so angry, I couldn't stand it anymore. I was tired of him hitting me.

I knew I would probably never be able to see Brenda again. Her parents didn't like me before, now they really had a reason to hate me.

Fuck them, fuck my dad, fuck everybody.

I was just gonna kill myself. I had nothing to live for anyway. I didn't give a fuck. So, as soon as everyone went to sleep, I was gonna take the car again because I still had the spare key, then smash into a light pole and commit suicide. That will show everyone. And not just any light pole. I was gonna crash into the one right in front of Brenda's house so her parents could see it. That was my plan, and nothing was gonna stop me.

I had to wait until 3 a.m. because that's how long it took for my mom and dad to fall asleep.

I pushed the car to the street again, but this time it wouldn't start. *What the fuck?* Then I knew as soon as I popped the hood. My dad had pulled off all the spark plug wires. Ha-ha, he thought he was fucking slick. *I'll show him.*

The car was only a four-cylinder, so I only needed four wires. I went to my moms Bel-Aire, took some wires off that, and put them on the Datsun.

I didn't know anything about firing order or how to put wires on correctly. I just put them on. The car started, but it sure ran like shit. It got me away from the house, but it was running terrible. I tried putting the wires on a different way, but it still ran like shit. I was just puttering along. I couldn't even get the car up to 30 mph. I wasn't gonna die going that fast, so I gave up, brought the car back home, went to my room, and cried, wondering what I was gonna do.

I knew for a fact that had my dad not taken those wires off, I would've smashed that car into the pole for sure.

From that night on, I was never allowed to use the car again. Brenda and I also broke up because it was just too hard to date each other. We just went our separate ways.

Chapter 49

I dreaded when report cards came out because I knew I would be getting all F's. I lost all interest in school. I just didn't see the point in it anymore.

Things at home started getting even worse with my dad, which was one of the reasons I didn't care about school because I knew I would run away again, especially if he kept hitting me, so I knew I would never finish school. Not only was I having problems with my dad, but I was also starting to fight a lot with my brother Joey. It seemed like he and my dad were both against me because one night me and my dad had gotten into the biggest fight we ever had, and when my dad chased me into my room to hit me, he couldn't get ahold of me like he wanted to, and my brother happened to be in the room and grabbed me and held my arms behind my back so my dad could hit me. That's when I just lost it.

I got myself away from them, ran across the room screaming, grabbed my phone, yanked it out of the wall, and threw it at my dad while screaming, "Get away from me, get the fuck away from me!"

That's when my dad just stared at me with the scariest eyes I ever saw. But I think I shocked him with my willingness to fight back, which I never had never done before. It was the first time I had actually hit him with something.

He just stared at me and said, "you're fucking sick," then left my room. I didn't know what to make of that comment. I was thinking that he must know about the flashing I've been doing for the past two years. That's the first thing I thought. Why else would he say I was fucking sick? That really scared me. If he and my mom knew, why haven't they said anything to me about it? Maybe I was just being paranoid. I didn't know.

After he left my room, I decided again that I was getting the hell outta that house. I was running away for good this time, so I waited about an hour, then went out to my van, and couldn't believe what I saw. All of my tires were flat. My dad had flattened all my tires. I couldn't fucking believe it. I was so pissed that I walked over to his car and flattened all of his. Now he was really gonna kill me. I then went back into my room and waited.

My dad knocked on my bedroom door, telling me there was a cop there to see me. There was a cop that lived down the street from us, so my dad had him come over and try to scare me.

My dad told him that I had flattened his tires and that I was uncontrollable.

That's when I said to the cop, "He flattened my tires first. Go look." I also told the cop that I was tired of my dad hitting me, but he wasn't even listening or believing me. He was totally on my dad's side. He then left, and I went back to my room.

A little while later, I looked out my bedroom window, which faced the front of the house, and saw my dad putting air back in his tires. He didn't even put any in mine. *Fucking asshole.*

I then came up with an idea. I would just wait until he goes to bed, steal his fucking car, and run away. He would never expect me to do that because I have never stolen his or my mom's car before, but that's what I'd do.

My dad left his keys on the kitchen counter like always, so I waited until around 1 a.m., grabbed them, then went out to his car, pushed it to the street, started it, then got the fuck away from there.

I had no idea where I was going. I didn't even have that much money. All I knew was I just wanted to get the hell away from my dad.

My first stop was a gas station to fill up. While I was filling up, I decided to go to my grandparents' house in Edgewater, which was close to New Smyrna Beach.

I ended up getting there around 2 a.m., so I decided to sleep in the car until later that morning, so I wouldn't scare them.

When I finally knocked on their door, they were very surprised to see me there all by myself.

I told them I stole my dad's car and ran away. Then they called my mom and told her I was there. I can't remember if my mom came and got me, or I drove the car back home, but my grandparents talked me out of running away and for me to let my dad have his car back.

I was back at home that day. I wasn't very good at running away and staying gone very long.

When I got home, my van was missing, and nobody would tell me where it was. Still to this day, I don't know what they did with it. I guess that was my punishment for running away and stealing my dad's car. So, there I was, without a car again.

Every time me and my dad and I would fight, he would chase me into my room and hit me, my mom was never in my room when he was attacking me. I would always tell her that he was hitting me, but she never seemed to believe me and would always stick up for him.

Then another time, he chased me into my room, I grabbed my aluminum baseball bat and told him to get the fuck away from me, or I would fucking hit him. He must have seen it in my eyes that I was dead serious because he left my room and went to tell my mom, and she couldn't believe it, saying to me, "How could you dare even think about hitting your poor father?"

"I'm sick and tired of him always hitting me," I said, and she still stood up for him. I couldn't believe it. I felt everyone was against me.

I'm pretty sure my grabbing that bat ended my beatings because my dad left me alone after that, but I still avoided him as much as possible.

Chapter 50

After breaking up with Brenda, I started dating a girl named Sarah, who Robert introduced me to. She was the first girl I dated who had her own car. She was also sixteen, lived about a mile away from me, and drove a Chevy Citation. Her parents were very strict. I couldn't even go to her house, let alone go into her room. That wasn't happening. So she would always have to drive over to my house at night. We would then sit in her car in my driveway and talk while listening to her sideways radio. Then we would kiss, have sex, and fog up the windows.

Our relationship didn't last long. I don't know why, but it seemed that every time I had a girlfriend, it had to be a secret. I hated that I always had to hide from their parents. Having girlfriends was cool because I liked to have sex with them—especially after having sex with Brenda, it felt good, and I wanted to have sex with every girl I could.

But it wasn't nearly as exciting as exposing myself. The adrenaline rush that flashing gave me is hard to describe. It was like being able to have sex with any girl I wanted because I got to pick and choose who I wanted to flash— like this one girl I saw in an apartment complex gym. She would've never let me have sex with her, but by me standing naked in front of her, and showing her how big and hard my dick was, then jacking off in front of her, and seeing the shocked look on her face, it was the greatest feeling in the world for me. It was just as good as having sex. It was like having sex without having sex, and it's what I would do for the rest of my life. I would look for the prettiest, sexiest, hottest girls I could find, girls that I knew wouldn't give me the time of day, then flash and jack off in front of them. That's all I could think about. It started at age fourteen and would continue to blossom out of control.

As you'll find out, it took over my life completely and destroyed everything that I ever tried to accomplish.

Chapter 51

It seemed like my dad was starting to be nicer to me, or at least trying to be, because one day, he asked if I wanted to go look at a car with him down the street that was for sale. It was a '72 Chevelle Malibu. The body was beat up pretty bad, and it was about five different shades of green, but the interior was really nice, and it ran great. The guy was only asking $300 for it.

My dad said that if he bought it, he and I could work on it together and fix it up. I knew he was just saying that. I was sure he was only thinking of buying it for himself. I still didn't trust him fully. He definitely wasn't gonna let me have it. I loved the car and saw the potential it had. My dad bought it, and we parked it on the side of our house. It wasn't registered, so we couldn't drive it. I helped him clean it up that first day, but as the weeks went by, my dad never did anything else with it; it just sat there, and we never did work on it like he promised.

So, I started fantasizing about it being mine. I sure would've loved to have it, so I started tinkering with it. I put my JVC stereo and pioneer speakers in it from the Datsun. And I remember the very first song that came on as soon as I hooked that stereo up. It was Dire Straits' "Money for Nothing." I sat on the side of the house, rocking out to that song, singing, "money for nothing and your chicks for free." Yeah, maybe my dad would give it to me; now that would be cool.

Things were going all right at home. My mom would get these really cool beer mirrors and neon beer lights from her store that the beer companies would give her, and she would let me have them to hang in my room. She also gave me all the beer posters that had girls on them. Me and my brother had a really cool room with neon lights, mirrors, and women everywhere.

One day, I came home from school and noticed that all my *Playboy* magazines were missing from the closet. Whoops, I guess my mom finally found them. I never asked her, and she never did say anything about them.

One thing I loved about my mom was her sense of humor. It was definitely where I got mine from. She was always making me laugh, doing funny stuff. She loved to pop her false teeth halfway out and chase me around the house. She would also put on scary Halloween masks and scare me; she loved doing that. So, one night I got her back really good. She had brought home a life-sized cardboard cutout of Elvira. Remember her? The mistress of the dark? It was so lifelike that when you first saw it, you thought it was real.

We had two separate phone lines in our house—one for the kids and one for my mom and dad. Ours was in our bedroom, and my mom and dad's was in the kitchen, so what I did was when my mom went to bed, I set up Elvira in the kitchen by the refrigerator facing her bedroom door, then I called the kitchen phone, so my mom had to come out of her room to answer it, and when she saw the Elvira standing there, she started screaming. It was so funny. I then came out of my room laughing so hard, saying, "Ha-ha. I got you; I got you."

Meanwhile, I guess my dad gave up on deciding to work on the Chevelle because he ended up giving it to me. I was so excited. No more bikes, go-karts, or dirt bikes. I was totally into cars now. I wanted to fix it up and make it nice.

We had some new neighbors that moved into my old girlfriend Cindy's house, and they had some really cool cars; one was a black Cobra II Mustang with gold stripes and racing stickers all over it, and the other was a green '67 Mustang. The Cobra looked like it was really fast. It was jacked up and had a big hood scoop and gold mag wheels on it.

One day, I saw them working on their cars, so I went over there to introduce myself. They were older than I was. The guy with the Cobra was in his twenties; his name was Dave, and the guy with the '67 Mustang was eighteen, and his name was Randy. They were brothers and lived there with their mom and dad.

Me and Randy hit it off pretty good. He knew a lot more about cars than I did and helped me work on mine when I had problems with it. We became friends and would work on our cars all day. I told him I wanted to fix my car up so it would go faster and look cool.

The first thing I did was put chrome valve stem caps on my wheels, which were really cool to have back then. One night, I spent the whole night stealing every one I could find in my neighborhood. I started collecting them to see how many I could get.

Then from there, I wanted to get chrome stuff for my engine. So, one night, I asked Randy if he wanted to drive around to all the used car lots after they were closed and look for cars that had souped-up motors in them, so we could take the parts off them and put them on our cars. He was all for it, so we went to all the lots looking for cars, and it didn't take us long. What was nice about the older muscle cars was you could pop the hoods from the outside, so we didn't have to worry about them being locked or not, which made it really easy. We would just pretend we were looking at them, and if there was nobody around, we would get the tools and start taking off any chrome or any other cool parts we could. But first, we made sure they were the same size motors as our cars, so we knew they would fit.

We found a '72 Chevelle just like mine, with a chromed-out motor, so I took the chrome Moroso valve covers, chrome air cleaners, chrome plug wire brackets, chrome braided wires and hoses, ACCELL Supercoils, and whatever else I could get off. It also had an Edelbrock manifold, Holley carburetor, and Blackjack headers. Randy had to help me get those because I didn't know how to get them off.

We were there for a long fucking time, trying to get all that shit off, but we got it all without getting caught. I couldn't believe we stayed so long, but it was definitely worth it.

We then put all the parts in Randy's trunk and went home. It was really late, so we just left everything in his trunk and went to bed for the night.

Me and Randy spent the following day putting all that stuff on our cars. I didn't want to put everything on my car at once because I didn't want my dad to find out and wonder how I got it all, so I just put a little on at a time. I started with just the valve covers and air cleaner, then left it like that for a while and kept the rest of the stuff in Randy's trunk.

Randy's brother's car was really fast; it was also the coolest car in the neighborhood, so I would always ask him if he could give me a ride in it. Back then, cruising was really popular and fun. We would just cruise through all the neighborhoods in Winter Springs and look for girls. The best time to cruise was around 5 p.m.

One day, Dave asked me if I wanted to go with him out to Highway 419 to see how fast his car would go.

"Hell yeah."

Highway 419 was the best place to go because there wasn't too much traffic on that road. It was a two-lane highway that went by the gravel place and Five Points baseball park. It was also the highway that took me to school.

We were in front of the gravel place, facing Five Points, toward Highway 17-92, when Dave came to a complete stop and said, "Are you ready?"

"Hell yeah."

He then punched it, smoking the tires and taking off. Then he put it into second gear and chirped the tires. Man, it was fast.

The next thing he said was, "look at the speedometer!" I think the speedometer went to 120 mph, but it was buried past that. *Wow!* Then he started to slow down. Man, that was fun. I'd never been in a car that fast before—even to this day.

I had a very busy sixteenth year of my life, especially once I got my Chevelle. That's when things started really going downhill in a hurry. I was stealing a lot more, mainly stuff for my car, just trying to make it look cool and go faster. I was also skipping school so much that I was never going to pass the ninth grade. I pretty much gave up on school and told my mom I was quitting. My older brother quit, so I figured, why couldn't I? So that's what I did.

I know my mom wasn't too happy, but it just didn't make any sense for me to go. It was a big waste of time, plus it was taking away from my flashing. I wanted to spend all day, every day, flashing girls, which was a lot more exciting than going to school.

Chapter 52

I continued to work on my car, trying to make it as nice as I could, so one night, I went to Kmart to check out their automotive section. I went there around 7 p.m. and found a really cool steering wheel grip. It was one of those things that I kinda wanted but really didn't want to buy, so I decided to just steal it. It was made of imitation leather, and you had to weave the fake leather string through the holes to put it on.

I wasn't a very good thief back then because I spent a lot of time in that aisle thinking about how I was gonna steal it. I was very nervous. The first thing I had to do was take it out of the box because the box was too big, so I did that, then I walked around a little bit more, thinking of what to do next. It was on the shelf and ready to go, but I didn't know where to put it because all I had on was a pair of jeans and a T-shirt. The only place I could think of to put it was down the front of my pants, so I did that and put the instructions in my back pocket. I then tried to see if I could walk without the grip being noticeable. Once I got it adjusted, I headed straight for the doors. I needed to get the hell out of there because I was really nervous.

As soon as I walked out the front doors, I heard the most dreaded words ever.

"Hey, excuse me."

Oh shit.

Before I even had a chance to run, a big lesbian grabbed me. I knew she had to be a lesbian because she looked like a bigger version of my Auntie Pat. She was huge. She had a buzz haircut, was wearing blue jeans, a flannel shirt, and had one of those wallets that bikers wore with a big-ass chain hooked to it. When she grabbed my arm, I didn't have a chance to even think about getting away. She was twice my size, so I just gave up. She then asked me to come back inside the store, that she just wanted to talk to me in her office.

She kept hold of my arm and led me through the store. Once we got to her office, she handcuffed one of my arms to a chair.

"What did I do?" I asked.

"You know what you did," she said. "Now, take that steering wheel grip out of the front of your pants."

So, I did that and handed it to her. Then she told me to give her the instructions that were in my back pocket. *Damn, she saw everything I did on camera.* So I gave her the instructions and asked if I was gonna get in trouble.

"Yes, the police on their way to the store to arrest you."

Oh no. I was so scared, I just knew my dad was gonna kill me and take my car away. So, I started crying.

"Please let me go. I will never do it again, I promise."

She said she couldn't because the police were already on their way.

"What about my car?" I asked. "What's gonna happen to it?"

She told me just to wait to see what the police wanted to do first.

The cops came and actually took me to the juvenile hall in Sanford. I'm not sure how long I stayed there, but they eventually released me to my mom, then gave me a date to appear in court for petit theft of the steering wheel grip. So, that was my very first arrest.

My mom had to get me a lawyer, and she wasn't too happy about that.

I ended up going to court, and they gave me probation with all kinds of rules I had to abide by, which really sucked because I found out I wasn't very good at following rules.

***

My mom and dad ended up taking my car away for two weeks, so I spent those two weeks working on it. My dad found that Edelbrock manifold and Holley carburetor in my trunk and wanted to know where I got them. I told him my friend Paul gave them to me, but I didn't think he believed me. I then went over to Randy's house and asked if he could help me put them on my car, so we spent the day doing that, and once we finished, my car never ran the same again. We just couldn't get it tuned right for some reason.

My car also had a crack in the windshield that I wanted to replace, so one weekend after I was finally allowed to drive again, I went around to all the junkyards and found a really nice one for $50. I learned how to put it in myself, but there was nobody around to help me. About ten minutes later, my brother's friend Tim came over. I really liked him because he was always so nice to me. I told him Joey wasn't home, then asked if he could help me put my windshield in because it took two people. I already had all the sticky adhesive stuff around the frame, so we both picked up the windshield and set it on the car perfectly. Then, after we put it in, we started going along the edges, pushing it down so it would stick to the rubber stuff. There must have been a tiny chip on the edge of the windshield on Tim's side because when he pushed on that spot, the windshield just cracked—and not a small crack either; it was over a foot long, right across the middle of the passenger side. I was so devastated that I ran into the house, straight to my room, started crying, and wouldn't come out. I stayed in there for two hours, just crying. I was so upset and mad at Tim that I didn't come out of my room until I knew he was gone.

I felt really bad later on because I knew he didn't mean to do it on purpose.

My mom even told me that he felt really bad and that he was sorry. I ended up seeing him a few days later and apologized for getting mad at him.

Now my car's windshield was worse than before, and it ran like shit, so I was really starting to give up on it. Maybe I could trade it for something else.

***

I found another job at a used car lot in Sanford, washing cars. Things were not going very well at home. I didn't like being on probation and having to follow so many rules, plus my car was running like shit. I was just getting frustrated with everything.

One day, I was over at Paul's house and told him that I wanted to trade my car for a different one and asked if he knew anybody who had a car they wanted to trade. He said he knew a guy who had a '75 Nova, so he called him, and the guy told us to come over and look at it.

I really liked the Nova. It had a better body on it than my car, but it only had a six-cylinder, which I didn't mind. The guy also liked my car, so we made an even trade. At least the Nova ran a lot better. We then exchanged titles, shook hands, and I drove away. I now had something new to work on.

***

While I was over at Robert's house showing him my new car, he told me that he and his friend Mark were going to New Orleans to watch the Chicago Bears in the Super Bowl. They didn't have tickets but were gonna try to sneak into the stadium. He asked if I wanted to go with them. It sounded fun, but I would have to run away and violate my probation.

I asked him whose car they were gonna take. Robert had bought an Oldsmobile Delta 88 that was really big, so he said they would drive that, and I could follow them in my car. I told him that I would have to wait until I got my paycheck from the car lot, so I would have enough money to get there. Then I decided, what the hell, I would run away and violate my probation. I didn't care, I wasn't happy at home anyways, plus I didn't like being on probation. So, I told him I would go.

Robert thought it would be better to take two cars in case one of us broke down.

Back then, gas was cheap, so it wouldn't take much money to get there. New Orleans wasn't that far away.

A few days later, we packed up our cars with everything we thought we would need, mostly just clothes and beer, then decided to leave that night around 9 p.m.

I met Robert and Mark over at Robert's house and told them not to get too far ahead of me. I told them if I flashed my lights at them to pull over because that would mean I was having problems with my car. My car didn't run that great, so I was kinda worried if it would even make it or not. They didn't have cellphones back then, so it was a lot harder to communicate.

We decided to take I-75 north to I-10, then take that west to New Orleans. We made it to I-75 with no problems, then my car started running like shit. I also noticed Robert and Mark were really pulling away from me, farther than normal, so I started flashing my lights at them to tell them to slow down a little. But they just kept going. Then my car started making all kinds of loud clanking noises, my oil light came on, and I really started getting nervous. So, I frantically started flashing my lights like crazy, trying to get their attention, but I knew in my heart they weren't gonna stop.

My car shut off completely, and I pulled off on the shoulder and started crying while banging on the steering wheel, cussing Robert and Mark out because I knew they were laughing and glad that I wasn't with them any longer. I waited for about an hour in hopes that they might come back, but I knew they were long gone and happy without me.

I was gonna have to leave the car there because it was blown up. I also knew I couldn't stick around sitting in it because I was now a runaway, and it would be just a matter of time before a Florida State Trooper came by and saw me sitting there.

It was too dark to hitchhike, so I needed to find a place where I could sleep until the morning, then I would hitchhike back home. I grabbed a blanket, got out of the car, waited for a few cars to pass by, then ran across I-75 to the southbound side, where I saw a building.

It was really fucking cold that night, so I was glad I had a blanket.

I walked up to the building and looked for a place I could sleep until the morning. It was around 11 p.m., so it would be a while before it got light out. I found a spot, curled up in my blanket, and cried again, thinking about how much my life sucked. I wished I had better friends that liked me. I guess I wasn't cool enough. It was also the second time Robert had done that to me. *Fuck him.*

***

I got a little sleep, but I tossed and turned all night because I was freezing my ass off. I left the blanket there and headed out to the interstate, stuck my thumb out, and got a ride pretty quick. *Wow!* That was really easy. I made it all the way home in four rides. It surprised me how easy it was to hitchhike and how nice people were.

When I got home, my mom told me the police were there looking for me. I couldn't understand how they could have come so quickly. I wasn't even gone that long. Then I knew my dad must have called them, saying I was uncontrollable or some other bullshit like that.

I wanted to run away again but decided to stick around for a few days. If I saw the cops come to the house, I would just run out the back door and through the woods. They would never catch me.

I remember the following day very clearly because my mom and I were out front in the driveway watching the Space Shuttle Challenger go up. Cape Canaveral in Titusville was not that far from Winter Springs, so we could watch the shuttles go up from our house. The Challenger blew up that day, and I remember my mom freaking out, saying, "Oh my God, oh my God," as she was crying. I didn't know what was going on until she told me. All I thought was that they would be fine because they probably had parachutes, but my mom knew better.

I was getting real paranoid being at home, knowing the police were looking for me, so I would go for walks. One night around 8 p.m. I decided to go to Afcom just to see who was there. I saw all the lights on, I knew the Puerto Rican girls didn't work there anymore, but I saw two cars in the parking lot and was just curious to see who was in there, so I looked in the front windows and didn't see anyone. Then I went around back to where the loading dock was because they had some windows back there too. I had all my clothes on. I wasn't jacking off or anything. I just wanted to see who was in there. I finally saw a woman who was old and ugly.

Hell no. I wasn't even gonna waste my time flashing her. I'd flashed old ladies before, but I had raised my standards and was only flashing hot chicks from then on, especially college girls—they were my favorites.

I was getting ready to leave when all of a sudden, I saw a Casselberry cop car sneak up on me out of nowhere. *Holy shit.* I couldn't even run. He had me trapped in the loading dock. Thank God I wasn't naked and jacking off, but he saw me leaving the windows, jumped out of his car, and yelled, "Freeze! Don't move!" His gun was out, pointed right at me. I was terrified as he told me to walk toward him. I was so scared because the parking lot was very dark and there was nobody else around. What he did next really traumatized me. He stuck his gun right in my face and said, "I will fucking kill you! That's my wife in there! What the fuck are you doing looking in those windows?"

All I remember is how big the hole in the barrel of that gun looked. I was shaking, telling him, "I wasn't doing anything, I wasn't looking at nobody, I was just looking for wood to build my fort with." There were a lot of wooden pallets around the loading dock, but he didn't believe me. He kept his gun on me. I have never been so scared in my life. He then told me I was under arrest for trespassing. Thank God he never mentioned anything about any of the flashings I had been doing there for the past two years. I guess the cops were never called in any of those cases because it was never brought up, but he did charge me with trespassing. Now I knew I was gonna spend time in juvenile hall.—not only for trespassing but also for violating probation, being an uncontrollable child, and running away.

***

I'm not sure how long I spent in juvenile hall, but it wasn't too bad. At least there were girls there that we got to watch TV and go to the recreation yard with. It was actually fun. Everybody would pick a girl they liked, and we would write notes back and forth to them. It didn't seem like punishment to me.

At night we would have to lock ourselves in a cell. I shared one with three other boys around my age.

Even though I didn't mind being there, we always talked about escaping. One night we decided we would try to break out the window and escape that way. The windows were about four feet tall and five inches wide, with a lot of black gooey stuff around them that looked like the same stuff that I used to put the windshield on my Chevelle. We figured if we could dig all of that out, the window would fall out, so we worked on that every night, just digging away. We got so much of it out that the window got very loose, but it just wouldn't fall all the way out. That's when we saw that the steel frame around the window was preventing the window from falling out.

Around this time, the guards saw us messing with it, then came into the cell and saw how loose the window was. They knew what we were trying to do, so we all got punished for damaging the window and trying to escape.

We told the guards that there was no way we could have got it all the way out. Getting it loose was all we could do. Oh well, I think our punishment was that we couldn't watch movies with the girls for a week, or something like that.

We also had counselors talk to us all the time. One of them said that nine out of ten of us kids were gonna end up in prison. He sure was right about me.

At night we would all have to take showers together. It was crazy. I wasn't afraid to masturbate and jack off in front of girls or have sex with them, but I was scared to take my underwear off in the shower in front of a bunch of boys my age because I was too shy and embarrassed. I didn't want anybody to see my dick. Explain that one.

One thing I would catch myself doing was looking at the other kids' dicks to compare mine to theirs. I wanted to see if mine was bigger. I wouldn't make it look obvious; I would just sneak a peek every chance I got. The other kids weren't shy at all. They would all walk around the shower area all naked, and there I was, wearing my soaking-wet underwear, I would even dry off with them on, then wrap a towel around me before taking them off, then put my dry under-wear on and get dressed without anyone seeing me naked. Weird, huh?

***

I ended up going to court for all of my charges and got sentenced to a group home, which was basically a foster home in Panama City, where I would be living with an older married couple. There would also be another kid living there with me. I was considered an uncontrollable child, and they figured it would help me to go live in another home for a while. I had to live there for six months.

It was a house in a regular neighborhood. The husband and wife were very nice; they were in their late fifties. They told me I didn't have to worry about clothes or anything. They would provide everything I needed. Then they showed me my room that I had to share with another boy around my same age. They also gave me chores that I had to do while I was there. It was just the other boy and me at that time, but they said they had room for two more kids. I was also told that if I was good for thirty days, I would be allowed to take a Greyhound bus home and visit my family for a week, so I looked forward to that. They were really nice and cooked nice meals every night. The husband also took us hunting and fishing. I also learned how to scuba dive while I was there, but I was getting really horny and missed being home looking for places to flash. That's all I could think about while I was there, so that's why I really behaved for the first month. I just wanted to go home and go to that apartment complex by my house. But I had to do something in the meantime to hold me over.

One night, when my roommate and I were in our room, he was showing me pictures of his girlfriend. *Wow!* I couldn't believe how fine she was. She had long blonde hair and was lying by a pool in a bikini, which gave me an idea: Later on when he wasn't in the room, I would take that picture into the bathroom and jack off to it. That's all I could think of to do, to satisfy my desire, so when he left the room, that's what I did and continued to do every night, and he never found out or caught me. That's what held me over until I could get back home.

Chapter 53

I was at the foster home for a month and was finally allowed to go home for a week, so they took me to the Greyhound station to catch a bus to Orlando, where my mom was waiting to pick me up. My mom and I always got along well, so on my first day back, I went to her store to help her and saw that she had hired a new girl named Pam, who was in her twenties, who was really cool and not too bad looking, so I decided to hang out even longer than I planned.

Pam was married, and her husband would come pick her up and drop her off at the store. I also found out she liked to drink because every day, when she got off work, she would leave with a case of beer. This made me come up with a plan. I think I had a plan; I wasn't quite sure yet, but I had a feeling that Pam liked me.

***

After months of waiting, I was finally able to get back to the apartment complex by my house. I was there bright and early the following morning after getting back from Panama City.

It felt so good to finally be able to look for women to flash again.

I got there really early in the morning, and the first thing I saw were three teenage girls walking in between the gym and the mailboxes. I watched them from a distance to see where they went when all of a sudden, they stopped on a corner, which was their bus stop, because not even ten minutes later, a school bus picked them up. Oh my God, you can just imagine how excited I was and the thoughts that were going through my mind as I looked at my watch and remembered the time. I definitely had to flash them before I went back to Panama City. I couldn't do it that day because they got on their bus too damn fast; I wasn't ready. After they left, I went and hung out in the gym, where nobody could see me. I didn't want to look suspicious while I looked for girls. The gym was the perfect spot because I could look out the windows and see everything going on outside; I especially got a good view of the pool and laundry room.

I was waiting for a girl to sunbathe, work out, or do her laundry. Any one of those three, and I didn't even care if they recognized me or not because I figured I would be going back to Panama City for another five months anyway, so I was ready to flash the hottest girl I could find, which I knew wouldn't take long, especially around there.

***

It didn't take long for my dream to come true. I was still at the apartment complex around 12 p.m. when I heard the gate to the pool slam shut. I was in the laundry room at the time, where I could also see the pool area. Oh my God, my heart started racing like crazy; I couldn't fucking believe what I was seeing. A girl in her early twenties was going to one of the lounge chairs by the pool to sunbathe, and she was fucking hot. She was wearing shorts and a bikini top. Oh my God, I couldn't believe my luck. She then spread out a towel on the chair and took off her shorts. Holy shit, she had a nice fucking ass; then she laid down and started putting suntan oil all over her body. I really couldn't believe what was happening.

I didn't know what nationality she was. She looked like she was half black, half white, with really long, straight black hair. *Wow*! She was so pretty and was also all by herself; there was nobody else in the pool area.

I took my lotion out of my pocket, pulled my dick out, and started masturbating like crazy with excitement, wondering how I was gonna flash her.

She was lying on her stomach with her head facing the other way when I came up with a crazy idea. I would walk out there without her seeing me, jack off next to her, cum all over her ass, then take off running—especially the way she was laying, she wouldn't even see me. *Yeah, that's what I would do.* But I needed to hurry before she rolled back over.

I had my dick all out in the laundry room and put more lotion on it. I couldn't take my pants all the way off; that would be too risky. Someone could come out of nowhere from any direction. So I held my pants up with my left hand while jacking off with my right as I was walking out there.

I approached her without her knowing, then not even five seconds later, I heard the pool gate, looked up, and saw a guy coming to the pool. Fuck, I pulled up and buttoned my pants really quick and started walking back to the laundry room as fast as I could. Oh my God, I had no idea if he saw me or not, so when I got back into the laundry room, I looked out the window toward the pool and breathed a sigh of relief. Thank God he didn't see what I was doing. I couldn't believe it. I went from being completely scared to death a few seconds prior to being completely pissed off when I saw what the guy did next.

All of a sudden, he wanted to come spend the day at the pool. Fuck, he damn sure fucked my whole day up, but after thinking about it, it probably wasn't a very bright idea to jack off on a girl's ass. It was one thing to flash her, but it would have been a lot more serious to have done something like that. I believe everything happens for a reason. The guy coming when he did probably saved me from getting into serious trouble because I was seconds away from cumming all over her sexy body.

I also took that as a sign I was definitely done for the day. I would just come back the following morning and get the girls at the bus stop. There was nothing that was gonna stop that. If I could get three girls at once, that would be cool.

From that day on, I loved going to apartment complex pools to look for girls sunbathing; they became one of my favorite places to look for girls.

***

I made sure I was at the apartment complex early enough to flash the girls while they were standing at the bus stop. The gym was the perfect spot to hide while I waited on them.

As soon as the girls showed up, I would make sure no cars were coming, then just walk right up to them, pull my pants down to the middle of my thighs, and show them my big hard dick.

Yep, that was my plan.

I looked at my watch, and just like clockwork, I saw them walking toward the bus stop. They were the same girls from the day before. *Hell yeah*. I knew I had to hurry and make it quick because the bus was coming. My dick had already been hard for over an hour, so all I had to do was make sure the coast was clear before I walked out there. My adrenaline was pumping big time; it was so exciting, just knowing I was gonna flash them no matter what.

I said to myself, *Here goes nothing*, as I walked right up to them, pulled my pants down, and asked them if they wanted to suck it.

It was crazy because that was the same thing that man in the woods said to me when I was seven years old. Now there I was, saying the same thing to girls while flashing them.

As soon as they saw me, all hell broke loose. They all took off running and screaming in every direction; backpacks and books were flying everywhere. *Holy shit!* I wasn't expecting such a big scene. I had to run like hell to get away from there. To make matters worse, they were running in the direction that I needed to go to get away from them. They didn't realize I was more scared of them than they were of me. I ran like hell in between the apartments and got away from there without getting caught. I'm pretty sure they missed their bus that morning.

I definitely needed to go home and chill out. I wasn't going back there again. That was satisfying enough to hold me over for a while. I would just kick it at my mom's store and hang out with Pam. I still think she liked me. Maybe she wanted some young dick. Her husband probably wasn't satisfying her, plus I had never been with a girl that old. She was twenty-seven, and I had just turned seventeen.

***

I went to my mom's store, and my suspicions were true. Pam asked me if I would help her stock the cooler, and as soon as we got back there, she grabbed my dick through my pants and said, "Whoops, I'm sorry," then gave me a hug and didn't seem to want to let me go. So I started running my fingers through her long hair. Then we started kissing.

As we were kissing, the bell rang, meaning there was a customer. There was a little rubber hose outside; when cars ran over it, a bell rang, letting us know someone was out there.

Pam waited on the customer; then, I told her we had to finish stocking the cooler. So we went to the back, out of sight from anyone, and started kissing again. This time she reached down and started rubbing and feeling my dick through my pants, feeling how hard I was while whispering in my ear, "I want some of this."

Then the fucking bell rang again and again.

Goddamn. That time, I had to stay in the back because my hard-on was too noticeable. I had to wait for it to go down. Then she got a mad rush of customers, so we never had a chance to do anything else before she had to leave for the day because her husband was on his way to pick her up. But before she left, she asked me what I was doing later that day because she had access to her car. So, we agreed to meet in the parking lot of the golf course across the street from the store.

***

Pam picked me up at the golf course with a six-pack of Budweiser, asking if I knew of a good place we could drink. I told her about a park on Moss Road that wasn't too far away, so we went there and started drinking. We both knew what we were there for, so after a few beers, we started kissing, and I started feeling all over her tits and ass. Then she stopped kissing me, unbuttoned my pants, pulled down my zipper, pulled out my dick, and started sucking on it. *Wow!* She definitely had experience because she was really good at it. After a few minutes, I couldn't take anymore. I wanted to have sex with her really bad.

We got into the backseat, but we had to make it kinda fast because she needed to get the car back home so her husband could take it to his job. She didn't have to worry about me taking long because when I helped her take off her jeans and panties, her pussy was soaking wet, so I just slid right in and went to town. *Damn*, her pussy felt good. She then asked if I could pull out before I came because she didn't need to get pregnant, which I preferred anyway. I wanted her to watch me cum all over her tits and stomach.

After she watched me come, we kissed one last time before she had to go.

We definitely couldn't let anyone see us together, so she dropped me off at the golf course, and I told her I would come by the store the following day to see her, which would also be my last day before I had to go back to Panama City.

***

It was my last day at home before I had to catch the Greyhound back to Panama City. I had to be at the bus station at 8 p.m., So I went to the store to see Pam and saw that her husband's blue '76 Monte Carlo was there. He was in the store hanging out, talking to Pam, so I introduced myself. We had never officially met. I would just see him picking up Pam from the store. He was pretty cool. I started talking about his car, so we went out to look at it, and he started tinkering with it. He then asked me if I wanted to go drink a few beers at his house. I told him I could, but I had to be at the bus station at 8 o'clock. I asked him if he could take me there, and he said he would, so I called my mom and told her she didn't have to take me, that I had a ride.

We then went to his apartment and started drinking and having a good time. Then, after a few beers, we went cruising around in his car. Only if he knew that I fucked his wife and got a blow job in his car just the day before.

Eight o'clock was approaching pretty fast, and I had every intention of going back to the foster home. It wasn't too bad there. But the more I drank, the more I started having doubts about going back.

We were cruising around listening to the Eagles' "Hotel California" and feeling fucking good. I think it was after about my tenth beer that I said, "Fuck that group home; I ain't going back." And that was it. I ended up staying with him and Pam that night, and when I got up the next morning all hung over, I was disgusted with myself. Damn, now what was I gonna do?

How do I explain this to my mom? I really wanted to go back to the group home, but it was too late. I had to go on the run again.

Chapter 54

I ended up getting sent back to juvenile hall for running away from the group home. When I went to court, they wouldn't send me back to the group home. Instead, they sent me to a place called Alligator Creek Stop Camp, up by Florida State Prison. It was a thirty-day program that consisted of chopping down trees, using swing blades, clearing brush, and carrying logs. It was like a military boot camp designed to teach discipline and how to be a man. It was funny because I had to do five more months at the group home, but by me running away from there, I got less time. I would now be home in thirty days. I could do that, but the only thing that sucked was that I would still be on probation afterward, which I fucking hated. I couldn't stand probation and being told what to do. But a little thirty-day boot camp would be easy.

At Alligator Creek, there were about six cabins in the woods with about ten boys in each one.

It was an all-boys camp. The food was really good, and we could eat all we wanted. They also had a weight set we could use to work out. I figured, by chopping down trees with axes, digging holes with shovels, and carrying logs, I might as well look at it like a thirty-day workout plan and start working out. I might as well try to get big muscles while I was there.

It was also the first time I ever saw an openly gay boy. He was in another cabin, but I would see him during the day. He never came on to anybody, but we all knew he was gay by the way he talked and acted.

They had an automotive class that would teach us how to rebuild an engine. I was really excited about that, so I signed up for it. They had a Ford 351 motor, and the teacher said he would teach us how to rebuild it. I couldn't wait, but as the days kept going by, the teacher kept making excuses. I could tell that he didn't really want to show us, he was lazy, and it would be too much work for him, so he ended up lying to me and the rest of the kids, which was really fucked up.

Like I've mentioned before, don't lie to kids. They remember that shit. If you say you're gonna do something, fucking do it.

I have tried my entire life to stick with what I say and to be a man of my word because I hate fucking being lied to.

I completed the camp without any problems, but I was still on probation for like five years or some crazy amount of time like that. I went back home, and things were going okay, except the only thing that sucked was I didn't have a car.

I started to notice my mom and dad fighting a lot around this time. Whenever they would fight, my dad would always go for a walk or take off in his car, staying gone for hours at a time. It was getting close to Christmas, and their fighting was escalating more and more. Then one day, my dad never came home, and my mom told us that he wasn't coming back. *Wow!* That was crazy, especially since it was so close to Christmas. I didn't know about my other brothers and sisters, but I was happy. I knew it was because of his drinking; it had to be. It would end up being years before I ever saw him again.

On Christmas Day, a big truck pulled up to our house, and these people got out and said they were from our church and had some toys to drop off for all of us kids. Somehow they found out about my dad leaving my mom with seven kids right before Christmas and felt they had to do something to help. I will never forget that day because my mom just stood in our front yard and cried, telling them they didn't have to do what they were doing.

***

My mom hired a new lady at her store named Beverly. She was an older lady—a few years older than my mom. I was talking to her one day, and she asked how old I was. I said I was seventeen, and she said she had a son a year older and would introduce me to him. So, the following week, he came to the store, and I got to meet him. His name was John, and he drove a red Ford Pinto. We hit it off pretty good. He took me to his house that day to show me where he lived in Casselberry. He liked to work on car stereos, so I helped him put a new stereo in his car. While we were doing that, he asked if I liked to drink, as he was grabbing some beers that he had in his car, so we started drinking in his garage and had a good time. We became friends and started hanging out.

The following day, he asked if I wanted to go to Daytona Beach to cruise and look for girls. He looked like he was twenty-one and never had a problem buying beer. I looked like I was fourteen, so I never even tried. Before we left for Daytona, he bought a twelve-pack of Old Milwaukee, which was the cheapest beer at that time. It wasn't too bad. We started drinking on our way to Daytona.

Back then, drinking and driving was the cool thing to do. It was illegal, I'm sure, but it seemed like everyone was doing it, especially teenagers. So we drove all over Daytona getting drunk as hell. I didn't understand how we never got pulled over because John was a horrible drunk driver. He would swerve all over the damn place. We even got lost a few times, but we had a good time. We never did find any girls and eventually made it home in one piece.

A few days later, I went over to his house, and he asked if I wanted to go to California with him. He said they were having the Super Bowl in Pasadena, and he wanted to go to all the tailgate parties in the parking lot of the Rose Bowl.

There was just one problem. We didn't have any money, so I asked him how we were gonna get there, and he said we could steal gas and food the whole way. I just laughed and said, "Are you serious?"

It would mean that I would have to run away and violate my probation again. John was eighteen and didn't have to run away. He could do what he wanted. I would be the one getting in trouble, but it sure sounded like fun. I told him there was no way his little Pinto would make it all the way to California. We needed a better car; that's when he said he could steal his sister Susan's car. She had a Dodge Omni that ran a lot better than his Pinto and was a lot more re-liable, So we decided to steal his poor sister's car that night, which would give us plenty of time to make it to the Super Bowl because it was just the beginning of January.

John and I left around midnight because we had to wait for his sister to go to bed.

We then took Highway 434 west to Interstate 4, then took that east to I-95 to Daytona, then took I-95 north. When we reached Jacksonville, we looked at a map and saw that if we took I-10 west, it would take us all the way to Los Angeles, but John said he wanted to get out of Florida as soon as possible, so we stayed on 95 north so we would be in Georgia really quick, instead of driving all the way across the Florida panhandle. Once we got into Georgia, we decided to just go north instead. We wanted to go to New York, Massachusetts, and Vermont to see some snow; then, we would head west across the top of the United States. We had more than enough time to get to California before the Super Bowl, so that's what we decided to do.

When we got to Georgia, we had to steal our first tank of gas. Back then, you never had to pay for gas first. They would let you pump; then you would go into the store and pay, so stealing gas was very easy. Trying to get away was the hard part. That's what we were most worried about. Our first attempt went smoothly. John would sit in the car, and I would pump the gas, then when I was finished pumping, I would get back in the car and say, "go, go, go, get the hell outta here." We would both be laughing and scared at the same time. We had a twenty-mile rule. Once we were twenty miles away from the gas station, we knew we were safe.

We then decided we needed beer, so I asked him how we planned on stealing that. We both decided that we needed to find a store where an old lady or old man was working by themselves or any girl. We didn't want anybody working that could chase us. Then we would have to park several blocks away so they couldn't get a description of our car. Our plan was to steal four twelve-packs apiece. We would put one under each of our arms, then one in each of our hands. That way, we would have enough to last us for a while.

We then found the perfect store where an old lady was working all by herself. We parked a few blocks away, and when we got into the store, we started laughing because it was such a perfect opportunity. We were the only ones in the store. We then grabbed our twelve-packs and started walking toward the counter, still laughing because we knew what we were getting ready to do.

We walked right by the counter, and we both said "bye" to the cashier at the same time as she yelled, "Hey, wait," and we were gone.

We ended up making it safely to the car and getting away. Mission accomplished.

***

John and I both saw snow for the first time in Vermont, where it was snowing like crazy. One great advantage we loved about the snow was when we did our gas runs, the snow was so heavy that it was all over our back bumper, which was perfect for covering up our Florida license plate, which helped us in our getaways.

While in Vermont, we started to realize that our feet were freezing with our sneakers on, so we went looking for a shoe store so we could steal some warm winter boots, and we ended up finding the perfect store. We saw a girl working in there all by herself. We then parked the car a few blocks away because we knew we would be running away from there.

Also, when I saw the girl all by herself and how pretty she was, it triggered something inside of me. All kinds of thoughts started running through my mind like I wished I wasn't with John. I also thought it would be a good way to flash a girl. I never thought of going inside a store.

I saw the way the aisles were set up and all the privacy they offered, but I put those thoughts aside because John and I were on a mission.

We went right to the men's aisle. The girl asked us if we needed any help, and we told her we were just looking.

John ended up finding a pair he liked that looked like Ugg boots, with all the wool on the inside. I also found a pair that I wanted. As we were trying them on, we couldn't believe our luck. The girl went into a room in the back of the store, and we decided, right then and there, we needed to get the hell outta there, so we put our old raggedy tennis shoes in the boot boxes, put them on the shelves, and walked right out the front door with our new boots on, without the girl even knowing we left. *Wow!* That was easy.

Now we had warm feet, and I also had a future plan.

We finally decided to start heading west. We had enough of the cold and freezing our asses off.

We would usually sleep at rest areas on the interstate and keep the car running with the heater on full blast to stay warm.

If you ever want to know if you are compatible with someone, take a trip across the country in a car with them, then you will know for sure, as I was beginning to find out. The stress of not knowing where our next tank of gas, meal, or beer was gonna come from also added to that tension.

I don't know how in the hell we did it, but we made it to Vermont, then all the way across the United States to California, stealing gas, beer, and food, the entire way while being drunk as hell. It was amazing.

***

They didn't have GPS back in 1987, so we had to find Pasadena by looking at a paper map.

Once we found the stadium, we were cruising through the parking lot and noticed a small building that looked like a restroom, so we stopped and saw that it was a restroom and decided that we might as well get cleaned up. So I grabbed a little bag with all my hygiene stuff in it and went into the bathroom. John said he would go after me because he wanted to finish his beer. I was probably in there for about ten minutes and came out to a very big surprise. John was gone. The fucking cocksucker just left me there; I knew it instantly and just laughed. I knew we weren't getting along because of all the stress of our trip, but I never thought he would just leave me in California with just a T-shirt and a pair of jeans on. *Wow!* I was really gonna freeze my ass off that night, and I didn't have a penny to my name.

I didn't even know anyone in California, so I just went to the nearest curb, sat down, put my head in my hands, and just didn't know what I was gonna do. A car pulled up and scared the shit out of me. I didn't even know it was there until the driver beeped his horn to get my attention.

I looked up and saw a brand-new, silver Lincoln Continental driven by an older white guy in his late forties, early fifties, asking me if I was OK. "No, not really; my so-called friend just left me here." I then told him the whole story of us driving out there from Florida for the Super Bowl and about us having a few arguments, but I didn't expect him to leave me stranded.

He then asked if I was hungry and wanted something to eat. I told him that I didn't have any money, and he said, "Don't worry about it," so I figured, what the hell. What else was I gonna do? The guy seemed nice enough. I lied and told him I was eighteen, but I'm sure he didn't believe me because I looked like I was fourteen.

His name was Gary, and he lived there in Pasadena. He owned a trucking company and lived by himself in a one-bedroom apartment. I got in his car, and he took me to a restaurant, where I got to order a nice hot meal, and I didn't have to take off running afterward, which was a relief.

I thought he might be gay, but he sure didn't look or act like she was. He then told me I was welcome to stay with him for as long as I wanted, or at least until I could figure out what I wanted to do.

It had been a long time since I slept in a real bed or had a hot shower, so his offer sounded pretty damn good. So what if he might be gay. I didn't care. Nobody else seemed willing to help me.

When we got to his apartment, the first thing I wanted to do was take a shower. He said he had some clothes that might fit me, and if not, he would take me shopping to buy me some. *Wow!* He was pretty cool. He asked me if I smoked marijuana. "No, I just drink and have tried cocaine," I said. He then asked if I minded if he smoked it. "Of course not," I said. "I actually like the smell of it." He then went and got me an ice-cold Corona out of the fridge. *Hell yeah!* It's just what I needed after what I'd been through that day.

He had to go to work the following day and said I was welcome to stay in the apartment while he was gone, which sounded really nice. I just wanted to kick back, relax, watch TV, and recover from that long cross-country trip. Yep, it is just what I needed.

His couch pulled out to a bed. He said I was welcome to sleep on that, or I could sleep on his bed with him. I chose the couch. It was getting late, and all I wanted to do was sleep; I was so fucking tired, so he gave me some blankets and a pillow, then pulled the sofa bed out.

He had to get up early and promised he wouldn't wake me up and that he would just see me when he got home. I thanked him for letting me stay, then crashed out, but before I fell asleep, I thought he had to be gay. He just hadn't come on to me yet. Maybe he thought I was under-age, which I was, even though I told him I was eighteen.

I then made up my mind. If he wanted to suck my dick, I would let him. That wouldn't be a problem, but that's as far as I would go. I'm sure he would make a move on me soon enough; plus, he trusted me to stay at his house. He was doing so much for me, that's the least I could do. I'd never had a blowjob from a man before.

Chapter 55

I must have been really tired because I woke up around 11 a.m., looked in Gary's room, and he had gone to work. So I went into the kitchen, found some Raisin Bran, ate a big-ass bowl, turned on the TV, and just kicked back when all of a sudden, the phone rang and scared the shit out of me. I didn't know if I was supposed to answer it or not, so I just let it ring, then it stopped, then started ringing again. That's when I said "fuck it" and picked it up. It was Gary telling me that when he got home, he would take me shopping for clothes. He also told me to help myself to any food I could find in the house and that he would bring home some more beer.

After I hung up, I went to the fridge and grabbed a Corona. I might as well drink the last three while waiting.

I found MTV and started watching videos. A few of my favorite ones came on, and I thought about jacking off but decided I would just wait to see if Gary came on to me later. Maybe he would give me a blow job while I watched them.

Gary came home around 5 p.m. and took me shopping. The main things I needed were socks and underwear. But he got me a couple pairs of jeans and a couple shirts. When we got back home, he ordered us a large pizza. He sure was spoiling me. We were just kicking back, drinking beer, eating pizza, and he was smoking his weed. I just knew something was gonna happen that night.

Then, just as I predicted, after we both had about six beers a piece, he asked if I wanted a massage—which I would later find out was a gay guy's favorite tactic to use when they wanted to suck a dick. It seemed to work pretty good. Who doesn't want a massage? So I said, "Sure, why not?" We then went into his bedroom, where he turned on his TV and had something a lot better than MTV to watch.

He asked if I liked porn videos. I told him I'd never seen one. Then he asked if I wanted to watch a gay or straight one.

"I would rather see one with girls in it," I said.

Wow! I couldn't believe what I was seeing. He then told me to take my clothes off and lay face down on his bed.

I left my underwear on because I didn't feel comfortable getting completely naked.

When I laid down, he got some lotion out of his night-stand and put it all over my back, and it was fucking cold, so he went to warm it up.

While he was gone, I was watching this girl on the video deepthroating a guy, taking him all the way down her throat. Damn, that was fucking sexy. I wondered if Gary could do that.

My dick was already hard from watching the video when Gary came back with the warmed-up lotion, then continued to massage my back. It was also the first massage I had ever gotten. It sure felt good. He did my whole back, arms, legs, and feet without missing a spot.

Then came the moment of truth, when he said, "Time to roll over."

My dick had been rock-hard the whole time, but he had yet to see it. Now he was gonna see it for sure. I was so fucking horny, I didn't care. He could have it, so I rolled over, and the first thing he noticed was how big and hard I was through my underwear. That's when he said I could take my underwear off if I wanted to. He didn't have to ask me twice.

He made a comment on how big I was and started sucking it." What happened to my massage?" I asked. *Oh well, a blow job feels a lot better anyways.*

I was watching the video, imagining Gary was one of the girls. It was also the best blow job I ever had. I hadn't had that many, but it was way better than what any of my girlfriends had given me, and it was a man doing it. It didn't take me long to tell him he needed to stop or I was gonna end up cumming in his mouth, which would've been another first; I'd never cum from someone giving me a blow job, so he stopped and told me that he wanted to watch me jack off and see me cum. Now that wouldn't be a problem. I was good at that. He then went into the bathroom and got a towel and told me to jack off and cum onto that.

I then grabbed some of his lotion and started watching the porn while jacking off, and it didn't take me long, especially after I had him rewind the tape back to the scene where a pretty brunette was deepthroating a guy. *Wow!* From that day on, the deepthroating scenes were my favorite ones to watch. I also loved the scenes where the guys would cum all over the girls' faces.

I couldn't fucking believe how much I came. Even Gary made the comment that he's never seen someone cum so much.

That wasn't a bad first experience for me with a man. It was also the first time I learned how to hustle gay men. It wasn't really hustling. I was just giving them what they wanted, and in return, they gave me money, food, a place to stay, or whatever else I needed. It wasn't a bad tradeoff. I thought about it. I was getting paid to get my dick sucked. Can't beat that (no pun intended).

That experience also planted a seed in my head.

***

After a week of staying with Gary, I started to get antsy. I wanted to flash women and didn't like being cooped up all day. I started to feel like a sex slave, waiting for him to get home from work, so he could suck my dick.

Gary had given me 40 bucks, and I knew he kept money in his wallet, so I came up with a plan.

I decided that I would wait for him to go to bed, take all the money from his wallet, take his keys, then steal his car. My urge to flash was just too strong. The thought of that girl in the shoe store was constantly on my mind, so I wanted to find girls working in stores all alone and flash them that way. That's all I could think about.

I didn't know how much money Gary had or how far I could get, but I was leaving that night.

***

I got one last blow job for the road. I kinda felt bad, especially for what I was about to do because I hated to steal, but it was the only thing I could think of to do.

I couldn't go walking around looking for girls to flash. That would be a sure way to get busted. I needed a getaway vehicle, plus Gary's car was big enough to sleep in, so I would need to take some blankets and a pillow with me.

Around 12:30, I snuck into Gary's room, and went straight for his pants that were lying on the floor next to his bed, took all the cash out of his wallet, along with his keys, then I remembered he kept his weed on his dresser and decided I might as well grab that too. I could probably sell it for some extra gas money.

He had a lot more money than I was expecting, which gave me a total of $107. Not bad; that would get me a good distance away. I then went back into the living room and put all my clothes in a duffel bag, grabbed a couple of blankets and a pillow, then snuck out the front door as quietly as possible and headed for the car. There was no turning back now.

The car was far enough away, so I could start it without him hearing, plus it would be too heavy to push anyway. I then started it up and drove away.

I needed to get as far away from Pasadena as possible before Gary woke up, saw me missing, then called the police and reported his car stolen.

I got on the first freeway I saw and headed toward LA because I knew that was where Interstate 10 was. I decided to get the hell out of California and head back to Florida while flashing girls the whole way. At least that was my plan.

I hated being the only car on the road—at least that's what It felt likc at 1 a.m.

I was very relieved when I finally found 10 East. I was even more relieved when I saw that Gary had a full tank. *Hell yeah.* I needed all the gas I could get.

The next city I passed through was Palm Springs, then Indio, then a whole lot of desert, then Blythe, which was right on the California-Arizona border. But before I got into Blythe, I saw a sign that warned drivers not to pick up hitchhikers because there was a state prison nearby. I thought it was a really cool sign, but never would I have guessed that twenty-four years later, I would end up at that same exact prison.

Then I saw signs saying, "Arizona State line, all cars must stop." That's when I started to panic. Oh shit, I didn't know what to do. I wasn't expecting that, and I was in a stolen car that I hoped hadn't been reported yet. I panicked so much that I pulled over on the side of the freeway, reached for the glove box, grabbed everything out of there that had Gary's name on it, and shoved it all under the seat. I had never stolen a car, so I didn't know what I was doing. I was just so scared that I had to stop at a checkpoint. I didn't know what they were gonna do.

I must have looked really suspicious. All they would've had to do was look, and they could see me pulled over. I wasn't that far away. I was also trapped. I couldn't even turn around because there were no exits between me and the checkpoint. I had no choice but to go through and hope for the best.

I started driving toward the checkpoint, saying all kinds of Hail Marys and Our Fathers, begging God to please let me get through there. I was so fucking nervous as I approached a guy in a uniform that looked like a cop, and all that he asked me, was whether I had any fruits or nuts.

Or some crazy shit like that.

I said, "No."

Then he said, "OK, have a nice time in Arizona."

And that was it. I did all that panicking for nothing.

I knew I had to look suspicious, being so young and driving a brand-new Lincoln at that time of morning, but I made it through. *Whew, that was close.* I did not like that feeling at all. I needed to find a rest area so I could get some sleep.

I stopped at the very first rest area in Arizona, used the restroom, then climbed in the huge backseat, wrapped myself in the blankets, and crashed out, hoping and praying I didn't get any rude awakenings from the Arizona highway patrol. That would really suck. The rest area seemed like a good place to sleep because I blended in with all the other cars that were there, plus I was tired; I had a long night.

Chapter 56

I woke up to the Arizona sun beaming through the car windows. I looked out the window. *Oh Shit*, I was the only car at the rest area. That was not good. I was standing out big time. The parking lot was full when I got there earlier that morning. I looked at my watch and saw it was 11 a.m. Yeah, it was time to go. So I went to use the bathroom. I needed to get out of there before a cop came rolling through.

As I was driving away, I saw a man hitchhiking on the on-ramp that looked like an Indian, A real Native American. I'd never seen or met a real Indian before. He looked really clean and nice, so I decided, *What the hell. I'll give him a ride.* I pulled right next to him, asking him where he was going. He said, "Texas," so I told him to hop in, that I would give him a ride there.

We started talking. He liked my car and asked if it was mine. "Yeah, it's mine." I knew by the way he looked at me that he didn't believe me. I told him I was going back to Florida, where I was from. Then the conversation turned to drinking and drugs. I asked if he liked to do any of those, and he said he liked to drink and smoke weed. That's when I told him I had some weed, but I didn't smoke it. That got him all excited, so I told him to grab my duffel bag in the backseat, and he was really shocked at how much I had; it was a Ziploc sandwich baggie, over half-full. I told him he could go ahead and keep it, but there was one condition. He had to buy us some beer since I wasn't old enough. He was in his forties.

We then stopped at the next gas station/convenience store we saw and bought a twelve-pack of Budweiser. But before I started drinking, I stopped at a Burger King to get some food in my stomach, then off we went, headed to Texas. But first, we had to drive through New Mexico.

We were having a good time, listening to Lynyrd Skynyrd's "Free Bird" on the radio. *Yeah, we must be traveling on now.* That's how I felt: free as a bird. Might as well enjoy every minute because my freedom was gonna come to a screeching halt later that night.

***

The Indian and I spent that whole day drinking. We even had to stop and buy more beer. We were taking our sweet time, stopping at a few rest areas, just kicking back and hanging out. I was in no hurry to get to Florida, and he was in no hurry to get to Texas. I told him he could sleep in my car if we got too tired to drive, but we continued traveling on, making it to New Mexico. It was also getting late.

What happened next taught me the number-one rule when driving a stolen car. I would learn many more later, but the first rule I learned was don't drive late at night, especially after 11 p.m. You do not want to be the only car on the road. You want to do all your driving during the day, so you can blend in with everyone else and not stand out. Cops get very bored in the late evening and early morning hours, and you don't want to be the only car cruising through town. Staying on a freeway, not so bad, but cruising through a small town at 2 a.m. was not a good idea, as I was getting ready to find out.

***

I was getting low on gas and needed to find a station, so I pulled off the interstate into what looked like a ghost town. Everything was closed, and I was drunk as hell from drinking all day and was starting to get really paranoid because I was the only car on the road. All it would take was just one cop to see me, and I would get pulled over for sure. I needed to get back on the interstate, where I felt a lot safer, so I was trying to figure out how to get back on I-10.

I was on a frontage road trying to find the on-ramp when I passed an old gas station, and my biggest fear came true. A cop was sitting in that gas station parking lot with all his lights off, except his yellow parking lights. *Shit.* I knew he was gonna come after me, even though I didn't violate any traffic laws. Sure enough, his headlights came on. *Fuck, I knew it. Fuck, fuck, fuck.* The first thing Indian said to me was, "this car's not stolen, is it?"

"No, but we're both fucked up, and there's beer cans all over the car," I said. "We're through."

Now the cop was right on my ass, following me. I knew he was running the plates, and his siren would be coming on any second. Then, BAM, just like that, the siren started blaring, and I pulled over.

The cop came up to my window and told me and Indian that we needed to step out of the car and have a seat on the curb.

He asked if we'd been drinking, and Indian said that he was, and I said I wasn't.

The cop said the car had been reported stolen. I told him that I didn't steal it. A friend of mine in California let me borrow it.

He then searched the car and saw all the empty beer cans, then popped the trunk. I had no idea what was in there because I never did open it since I had the car. It was full of computer equipment. *Oh shit*. That didn't look good. Then I remembered Gary owned a trucking company, so I told the cop that they were for my friend's business, but he didn't believe a word I was saying, I could tell.

Then he said Indian and I had to take a sobriety test. By that time, another cop had pulled up, and I just knew we were going to jail. I failed at trying to walk a straight line. That wasn't happening. So, off to jail we went.

It was really strange because the cop never arrested us for anything. He just said we had to go to the police station and stay in the drunk tank until we sobered up, which I thought was weird. Why wasn't I getting arrested?

When we got to the police station, we were put into the same holding cell, even though I was seventeen and Indian was in his forties. All kinds of shit was running through my mind.

What were they gonna do with me? Were they just gonna let me go in the morning? I was trippin' out. I didn't know what was gonna happen.

Then, later that morning, a cop came and told Indian that he was free to go, so I shook his hand and said that it was nice to meet him. Now I was really nervous. How come they weren't letting me go? Then, ten minutes later, another cop came and got me, saying, "come with me."

"Where am I going?"

He wouldn't tell me. It was weird because he didn't even handcuff me as he brought me to his car and told me to get into the front seat. Now I was really tripping. I fucking flat-out stole a car, was drunk driving, and still hadn't been arrested. Now the cop was taking me to who-knows-where. He was a New Mexico state policeman, who got onto Interstate-10, then pulled off on the shoulder and told me to get out, that he didn't want to see me in his state again. *Wow!* I was in shock; I couldn't believe it.

All I had were the clothes on my back, a pair of jeans, and a T-shirt, but I didn't care. I was free. I couldn't fucking believe it. He was just letting me go.

Then afterward, I got to thinking I knew why. It was because of Gary. He must have thought about it really hard. He would have been foolish to press charges against me for stealing his car. He must have known I was under eighteen, and he was probably scared I would retaliate against him and tell the cops he sucked my dick. Then he would have been charged with having sex with a minor. I would've never done that. It didn't even cross my mind, but I'm sure he was terrified of something like that happening.

I'm sure he told the cops he didn't want to press charges, that he just wanted his car back or something like that. Otherwise, they wouldn't have just let me go like that, free and clear. Thanks, Gary, even though I would've never accused you of molesting me. I was a willing participant.

***

I was somewhere in New Mexico on Interstate-10. There was not much else I could do but hitchhike back to Florida, so I started walking along the shoulder of the interstate, which I knew was illegal. I had no idea why the cop would just drop me off there, but then again, a lot of things didn't make much sense within the past ten hours.

I walked to the next exit so I could get to an on-ramp, then I would just stick my thumb out and see what happened. At least I still had a little money and didn't have to pay for gas anymore. But I damn sure was gonna freeze my ass off at night. I didn't even have a jacket or a long-sleeved shirt to wear.

I was so fucking mad that the whole time I had the car, I didn't get to flash even one girl. I should've never picked up that Indian. I spent the whole time drinking with him and never got the chance to do the one thing I wanted to do the most. The only reason I stole the car was so I could flash. Never again will I pick up another hitchhiker.

As I was thinking of all that, a green Freightliner pulled over to give me a ride. *Hell yeah.* I hoped he was going far. I ran up to the passenger side, opened his door, and the driver told me to get in. *Wow!* It was the first semi that I ever got to ride in. It was really nice and had a big sleeper. The driver was an old man who said he was headed to Georgia but first had to stop in Texas for the night to sleep.

I told him the whole story of being left in California and that I was just trying to get back home to Florida. I left out the part about Gary and stealing his car. I didn't need to tell him that.

He said I was welcome to sleep in his truck in Texas; then, he would take me all the way to Georgia if I wanted. That sounded good to me. I was just thankful that I wouldn't have to spend the night on the side of the road, freezing my butt off. I didn't even want to think about that. Plus, I was so fucking tired, all I wanted to do was crawl into his sleeper and go to sleep, but I tried to stay awake and keep him company for as long as I could.

I told him I wanted to be a truck driver someday. I loved big trucks. It was also exciting for me to listen to all the truck drivers talking on their CBs. It seemed like it would be a fun and exciting job to have, traveling all over the country.

He let me talk on his CB and even gave me a handle.

He called me "Stud Muffin." I have no idea why he called me that. His name was "Ghost Rider."

I enjoyed talking to the other female truckers the most. We had a good time. He even took me to a truck stop somewhere in Texas and bought me biscuits and gravy.

We were 100 miles from where he needed to stop for the night, and there was no way I could stay up that much longer, so I asked him if I could crash out in his sleeper. As

soon as I laid down, I was out. I slept the whole 100 miles because I was woken up by the sound of the truck slowing down and coming to a stop, I was too tired to get up, so I pretended I was asleep because I wanted to continue sleeping throughout the night. I wanted to be nice and refreshed and back to normal by the morning. Then I thought about him climbing back there with me. The mattress wasn't very big. Two people could fit on it, but there wouldn't be a whole lot of extra room after that.

Those were the thoughts crossing my mind when the truck finally came to a complete stop.

I heard him set the air brakes, so I rolled over and faced the back wall, pretending I was asleep while trying to give him as much room as possible. I didn't want to get up. I was too warm and comfortable, plus I needed a lot more sleep; I was really tired.

I could hear him. He wasn't getting out of the truck. He was just sitting in the driver's seat. Then I heard him coming into the sleeper. I was just lying there frozen, feeling really weird and uncomfortable. I knew he wasn't gay because he had pictures of his wife and kids taped on his dashboard, but I was still nervous as hell as he crawled into the bed next to me. *Damn.* How was I gonna be able to get back to sleep? That's when he touched my butt and started rubbing on it. *OH, HELL NO!* I jumped straight up and yelled, "What are you doing?" and he said, "Oh, I'm sorry. I thought you were my wife."

"Yeah right, sure you did. I am getting out of here."

I was so pissed for two reasons: one, he wouldn't let me sleep, and two, I had to get out into the cold and freeze my ass off, and it was too late to hitchhike. I was so fucking mad.

He sure had me fooled. I would've never thought in a million years that he was gay.

I didn't know what I was gonna do for the rest of the night. The place he stopped at was just a parking area on the side of the highway; It wasn't even a truck stop. There wasn't any place I could go to hang out and keep warm. It was bullshit. *Fucking asshole, putting me out in the cold like that.* It fucking sucked; I was freezing my ass off. All I could do was walk to stay warm, so I went out to the interstate and stayed in between the east and westbound lanes, in the median, so no cars could see me. I also didn't want to get run over. I would walk until I got tired, then I would sit down until I got too cold, then start walking to warm back up. I did that all night for at least ten miles until it was finally daylight. I then found an on-ramp, stuck my thumb out, and hoped whoever picked me up was going all the way to Florida because I didn't want to have another night like that. That was not fun at all.

***

I was so fucking tired, I just wanted to find a truck stop. I remembered that driver telling me they had showers and TV rooms where drivers could relax and rest, so the next person who picked me up, I was just gonna tell them to take me to the nearest truck stop. I needed to recuperate and take a shower. I was too tired to keep someone company again. I just wanted to find someplace warm to sleep; then, I would hitchhike again when I was back to normal, whatever that meant.

I wasn't even standing on the on-ramp for fifteen minutes when another big rig stopped to give me a ride. That was easy. I ran up, opened the passenger door, got in, and told the driver I just wanted to go to the nearest truck stop.

I told the driver all about my last adventure with the truck driver who thought I was his wife.

It was so fucking crazy because as I was telling him that story, that driver was actually passing us on the highway. I couldn't believe it.

"There he is right there. I'll be fucking damned; speak of the devil."

Then the driver I was with got on his CB while asking me what his name was.

"Ghost Rider."

Then he says, "Hey, Ghost Rider, is that you?"

I heard Ghost Rider say, "Yeah, go ahead."

"Hey, I got your wife in my truck with me."

It was so fucking funny; I couldn't believe he said it. Ghost Rider must have shut his CB off after that because he didn't answer back. I knew that this driver wasn't gay because he didn't make any moves on me and took me to a truck stop, which worked out perfect because he wasn't going that much farther anyway.

He said I would have a good chance of getting a ride from there because they had a real busy on-ramp with lots of cars and trucks. It was also the perfect place for me to stop and get some rest.

It was only 11 a.m., but I was just too tired to continue. I was gonna try to sleep in the driver's lounge, get something hot to eat, take a shower, then continue hitchhiking in the morning.

Before pulling into the truck stop, I noticed a strip mall with a bunch of stores. It reminded me of the strip mall where John and I found that shoe store where we stole those boots.

That memory crossed my mind as we were pulling into the truck stop.

***

While I was sitting in the truck stop, I was thinking about how badly I wanted to expose myself to some girls. The urge was really strong, but I didn't have a fucking car, and it would be so hard to flash without one. How would I get away? It would be too risky. I didn't want to get arrested for that. What an embarrassing arrest that would be. What kind of person would do that? Me, of course. Then I remembered that strip mall and had an idea. I was gonna go over there and see if I could find a girl working in one of those stores I could flash. Then I could run back to the truck stop and hide in the driver's lounge. But first, I had to wait for it to get dark. That way, I wouldn't be seen as easily running away; plus, one thing I noticed about strip mall stores: it was a lot easier to see who was working in them at night because the stores were all lit up inside, and I could see who was in there without them seeing me. It was a lot harder to see who was in them during the day without walking directly into the store.

At this stage of my flashing, I was too scared to actually walk into a store and flash. I would escalate to that later, but right then, girls just seeing me naked outside their store windows was satisfying enough. So, that's what I would try to do as soon as it got dark.

****

It finally got dark enough that I could walk over to the strip mall, which ended up being farther away than I thought. I had to walk across a big open field; then, it was about four more blocks after that. I made it over there and noticed most of the stores were closed, and the ones that were open had men working in them, which fucking sucked.

The last store I looked into was a yogurt shop, and that's where I hit the jackpot. *Fuck yeah.* I couldn't believe what I saw when I looked in the windows. *Hell fuckin yeah.*

There were two teenage girls in there working all by themselves, with no guys in sight. *Yes, yes, yes.* The shop was also in the perfect location at the end of the strip mall. All I would have to do after I flashed them was run behind the mall, jump a fence, run a few blocks, then run across the field to the truck stop. It was a long run, but I could do it before the cops swarmed the area. At least I hoped I could. It was pretty risky, but I just had to do it, especially after seeing those girls all by themselves. I was so excited. I just hoped I had enough time before they closed.

I remembered that stores usually had what time they closed posted right on their door or window, so I walked up to take a look and saw that I had plenty of time. *Hell yeah.*

They were definitely gonna see a big hard dick before I left. I couldn't wait; I was already hard with anticipation.

I was ready to pull my dick out and start jacking off when all of a sudden, a pickup truck pulled right up to the front of the shop. A guy jumped out and went inside to get some yogurt.

He didn't even look at me, which was good. Then another car pulled up with a man and woman in it. All of a sudden, everybody wanted to eat yogurt. *Goddammit.* I couldn't do shit until all the customers left, especially the men, so I had no choice but to wait. I still had plenty of time to get them, so I walked away to a spot where I could still see the parking lot and waited for those customers to leave.

As soon as the customers left, I walked back over to the windows to where I could see the girls, but they couldn't see me. *Wow!* They were really cute; I was gonna get them both in one shot. I then pulled my dick out and started jacking off while watching them. I also made sure I wasn't visible from any cars pulling up and seeing me. All the other stores were closed by this time, and the parking lot was really dark except for the yogurt shop, which made it even better for me—hardly any traffic at all, so I was not too concerned about being seen by anyone.

The girls were behind the counter and too far away from the window where I wanted to flash them, so I needed to wait for them to come out to where all the tables were, so they would be able to see me better.

While I was waiting, another car pulled up. *Goddammit,* now I had to go for another walk until that car left.

I noticed some dumpsters off to the side and came up with a great idea, which would be a much better experience for me, and it would also shock the girls even more.

I would get completely naked behind the dumpsters, then walk up to the windows like that. *Hell yeah.* So, as I was waiting for that car to leave, I took all my clothes off.

The customer stayed in there forever, but when he finally left, one of the girls followed him to the door to let him out, then locked the door behind him. *Oh shit.* They were closing. I had to be quick, but at least I didn't have to worry about any more customers coming and fucking me up.

After that last customer pulled out of the parking lot, I walked up and saw one of the girls getting ready to mop the floor. *Hell yeah.* It was perfect because she would be very close to the windows. Then I saw the other girl start cleaning the tables. They were both out there together, very close to the windows. It was the perfect opportunity; I had to get them right then; it wasn't gonna get any better. Plus, they were getting ready to leave.

Hell yeah. I loved it. The adrenaline rush was amazing; I almost came before I even flashed them.

Just the excitement of knowing what I was gonna do made it so hard to keep from cumming, but I stopped my-self, then walked right up to the front window. The girl mopping saw me right away, and I could read her lips; she said, "OOOH MY GOD," then she told the other girl to look as I was waving my dick from side to side. Once the other girl saw me, I started jacking off while they were both look-ing. Then they ran behind the counter, and one of them got on the phone, but they were still watching me. I needed to get the fuck out of there, so I came all over the window while they watched, then ran like fucking hell. I had a long way to run, plus I had to put my clothes back on.

I was scared to death running back to the truck stop. I was even scared once I got there because I had to stay there until the morning. I'm glad I decided to get completely naked because I only had one set of clothes. A red shirt and blue jeans would've been real identifiable.

Now that was an adrenaline rush, better than cocaine, better than drinking, better than having sex with a girl, better than getting blow jobs, better than anything. Flashing had become my drug of choice, Period. It was the greatest feeling in the world for me and would continue to be for years to come. Nothing else would matter, NOTHING.

Chapter 57

I got a ride all way to Florida, where I-10 and I-75 came together, which was a really bad spot to get a ride from, so when the driver pulled over on the shoulder of I-10, I was cussing him out under my breath.

I had no choice but to start walking in search of an exit, hoping it would have a good on-ramp to hitchhike from. It was a pretty desolate area, so I kept my thumb out while walking, just in case; I never knew if someone could stop. Hopefully, it wouldn't be a cop. I'm sure I had a warrant for my arrest by then. It had been a while since I ran away with John, so I'm sure I've been reported missing.

Well, it didn't take long to confirm my suspicions when a cop in an unmarked car pulled up right behind me as I was walking down I-75, got out of his car, and asked where I was headed.

I told him I was going back to Winter Springs, where I was from. He then asked for my name, date of birth, and Social Security Number. That's when I decided to just give up. I wasn't even gonna try and lie. I was so drained and tired, I just wanted him to arrest and take me somewhere I could sleep. Plus, I was cold and hungry.

He called my name in on his radio, and it didn't take long. A warrant had been issued for my arrest. Whew, what a relief. Take me away.

He didn't put handcuffs on me. He just told me to get into his car, that he had to take me to the nearest substation, or jail, or whatever it was so he could contact Orlando, so they would come pick me up.

When we arrived at the station, I was put into a cell with a mattress and a blanket, hoping Orlando would take their sweet time because all I wanted to do was sleep as much as I could.

***

I ended up sleeping in the holding cell all night, which was really nice because I needed the sleep. The first thing in the morning, another unmarked police car came and picked me up.

I asked where he was taking me, and he said I had to go to the juvenile hall in Orlando for running away and violating my probation. Thank God I was still seventeen because I didn't want to go to an adult jail.

When I got to the juvenile hall, I was told I had to stay there until a judge could decide what to do with me. It was pretty much the same as Seminole County Juvenile Hall, except it was a lot bigger.

It wasn't too bad there. They also had girls we could talk to and pass notes to. It didn't seem like much punishment, not for me, anyway. Maybe it bothered the other kids, but it didn't bother me. It was like a vacation. I was just so tired of being on the run and hitchhiking that I needed a break.

When I finally went to court, I was sentenced to a juvenile halfway house for six months. I was kinda excited about that because I was almost eighteen and didn't want to go to jail. But I knew the next time I fucked up; I would be going to a county jail as an adult for sure.

***

I was sent to a place called Orange House, on Orange Blossom Trail (OBT) in Orlando, located on one of the most famous streets for prostitution at the time. It was also where all the adult bookstores and topless bars were.

What a perfect place to send a bunch of horny teenagers. The halfway house was smack dab in the middle of it all. It was an old motel converted into a halfway house. It didn't seem like much punishment to me. The only thing that sucked was that it was all boys, which they put two per room. It was pretty cool. My roommate was a black kid named Devin, who was the same age as me, so we became friends.

Every weekend we would have car washes out front. There was a lot of traffic on OBT. So we got a lot of business. We even got truck drivers who would pull in there.

Our biggest entertainment was seeing the prostitutes walk by. It seemed like a different one walked by every thirty minutes. We would always whistle and yell at them. It was the first time I ever saw a real prostitute. Every now and then, there would be one that wasn't too bad looking. Me and Devin would always say to each other, "yeah, I would do her," or "hell no, I wouldn't touch that one."

Neither one of us had ever been with a prostitute, but that was about to change.

***

The staff at the halfway house would give us day passes, but the passes were strictly to look for work only.

One night, me and Devin came up with a plan. We both wanted to have sex with a prostitute, so we pretended we were gonna look for a job and get a day pass, but instead, we were gonna look for a prostitute.

There was a motel three blocks away, where a lot of prostitutes hung out, so we decided to go there to see if we could find one that we both wanted to fuck, but we only had twenty bucks between the two of us, which we didn't even know if that would be enough or not, But we were gonna find out.

The next day, we got our passes and started walking toward that motel. We were both nervous and excited at the same time. I told Devin that I wasn't gonna fuck an ugly one. He wanted to fuck a white girl, so I agreed to that, even though I kinda wanted to fuck a black girl because I've never had one.

We would look for one that we both liked, then approach her and ask if we could both have sex with her for twenty dollars and just see what she says.

When we got to the motel, we hung out behind it, out of sight from the traffic on OBT, so none of the workers from the halfway house could drive by and see us because they would have known what we were up to.

We had a good view of the girls that were out front. We both spotted our girl walking to the Coke machine that was near the front of the motel. We both said, "look at that," at the same time. We wondered if she was even a prostitute because she was a lot better-looking than most of the ones we'd seen. "Come on, let's go find out." We tried to hurry and reach her before she went back into the room that she came out of.

When we reached her, I said, "Excuse me, are you working?"

"What's up? What do you need?"

"What can we get for twenty bucks? Me and my friend want to have sex with you."

"OK, I'll do both of you for twenty, but only one of you at a time, so one of you will have to wait outside."

Then she asked who wanted to go first? Me and Devin both looked at each other, and I told him he could go, I was scared to go first, but I didn't tell him that, so Devin went into the room with her while I hung out behind the motel and waited.

Devin wasn't gone long at all. He was in and out of there in less than twenty minutes." *Damn, that was quick.* Oh shit, now it was my turn. I guess I get sloppy seconds. I didn't even think about that when I let him go first. Oh well, I didn't care; I was getting some pussy. She would also be the oldest girl I've had sex with up until that point. She was in her thirties.

I went into her room and could tell she was a professional prostitute. She took control right away, telling me to go ahead and take my pants and underwear off, then she walked over to her purse and got a condom, then took all her clothes off. *Wow!* She had an alright-looking body. She came over to the bed and saw me playing with myself and told me she had to put a condom on me. It was also the first time I ever saw or used a condom. As she was putting it on me, she said, "Damn, you're bigger than your friend out there." Then she laid down on the bed and said, "I'm all yours."

I didn't waste any time; I dove right in and went to town. She even let me kiss her.

I couldn't make fun of Devin any longer because I was outta there in about twenty minutes also.

I then went outside and gave Devin a high five as we were walking away. That was cool.

I didn't tell him about the comment she made to me. I didn't want him to feel bad, so I kept that to myself. We then went back to the halfway house and told the staff that we looked everywhere and couldn't find a job. There was nothing really around there. We then went back to our room to shower and hang out.

Me and Devin both liked being there. It was cool, and not a whole lot of rules to go by, but we did have to be in our rooms at a certain time every night. We also had to go to group counseling during the day, along with school classes.

Another thing that was pretty cool was that they had a phone booth outside that we could use to call our family and friends. It was cool because we could go inside it and close the door, so it was nice and private.

Most of the boys would use it to call their girlfriends, so me and Devin were always asking them if they knew any girls that we could call. One of the boys said he knew a girl named Ashley I could call, then gave me her number. So I called her, and we hit it off right away and ended up talking every day. She was sixteen, and I had just turned eighteen.

I told her about my trip to California and how me and my ex-friend John stole his sister's car then stole gas, food, and beer, all the way there. I also told her how I hitchhiked back to Florida by myself. She thought that was the coolest thing and told me she always wanted to go to California and asked if maybe I could take her someday. *Hell yeah.* I told her that would be cool, but I first had to do five more months at the halfway house.

After weeks of talking to her, I called her one night, and she was really stressed out because she and her mom were fighting, and she told me she was thinking about running away with her friend Nicole. She was crying and asked if I would help them run away. She told me she would steal her mom's car and come pick me up, she would also have sex with me, and we could go to California. Well, that's all I needed to hear, so I guess I was gonna run away, just to get some pussy, Fuck it, I didn't care.

I told her that I would call her back to let her know what I already knew.

***

I went back to my room that night and thought about running away with Ashley and Nicole.

I also told Devin about it and asked if he wanted to go with me. He said, "Hell no, I'm cool."

He only had a month or two left before he went home, so I didn't blame him.

I would leave in the middle of the night. Our room was on the second floor of a two-story building. It would be too risky to walk out the front door in the middle of the night because they had staff members that worked at night and could see the front doors to all the rooms, so I went and looked out the back window and saw a big TV antenna right outside my window that came up from the ground that I could side down, which was the perfect escape route. *Hell yeah*. I also saw a mobile home park right next door. My plan was set in motion.

I called Ashley the next day and told her the plan and asked her what kind of car her mom had so I knew what to look for. I then told her about the trailer park I could see from my back window, so I told her to park right in front of that at midnight, and when I saw her car, I would climb out my window and meet her and Nicole there. I also asked how much money she and Nicole had, which was sixty bucks. That would at least get us out of Florida.

Ashley said she also had some beer they would bring, which made things even better.

We were all set. We were gonna do it that night.

I was really nervous leading up to my escape from the halfway house. I couldn't believe I was going on the run again, just to get some pussy. Maybe I could fuck both of them. That would be even better. I didn't even know how they looked.

Ashley described herself. She was skinny and had short blond hair. I had no idea how Nicole looked. But oh well, I would find out soon enough.

It was getting close to midnight, and Devin was laughing, telling me I was crazy.

As I was looking out the window, I saw them pull up in front of the trailer park. I said goodbye to Devin. "Wish me luck; I'm going to drink some beer and get some pussy." Then I climbed out the window, slid down the antenna, ran to my getaway car, and jumped in the backseat.

Wow! The first thing I noticed was how cute Ashley was and how hot Nicole was. *Damn*. This was gonna be fun.

The first thing I told them to do was find a gas station because they only had a quarter tank left.

After we filled up, we got on Interstate-4 headed toward Daytona.

We all popped open a beer and gave each other cheers, "to California."

Neither Ashley nor Nicole had ever been out of Florida, so it would be fun for me to show them the country.

The smartest thing we could do at that hour was to stop at a rest area. It was too risky to be driving around. I learned that lesson in New Mexico.

We found a small rest area between Orlando and Daytona. There were no restrooms or vending machines, but that was okay. We would just stay there and drink until later that morning when there would be more cars on the road so we wouldn't stand out so much.

When we stopped, Ashley gave me a hug and a long kiss. I also gave Nicole a hug. We all got out of the car and stretched, and that was when I got the first look at their bodies. Ashley was really skinny with no tits or ass. But Nicole, Wow! She had a body and was pretty. She had nice tits and a nice ass. *Oh my God.* She was also mixed with another race; she was either half Mexican or Puerto Rican and white. Damn, why couldn't she have been Ashley? Oh well, I would have to make a move on her at some point; I didn't really care because I knew as soon as we got pulled over, it was a wrap. I would be off to a county jail and would never see either one of them again.

I thought about getting a motel room and having a threesome. Now that would be worth it before we got pulled over. I wondered if they would go for that. Then I decided against it because that would take all the money we had, so I would just have to settle on trying to fuck them in the car. I also wanted to get as far away from Florida as possible.

We stayed at the rest area until the sun came up, then headed toward Daytona so we could get on I-95 and start heading north toward Jacksonville, where we would then get on I-10 west and take that all the way to California. At least that was the quickest way to California, but when we got to Jacksonville, I decided to do the same thing that me and John did months earlier. I wanted to get out of Florida as soon as possible, so we stayed on I-95 north because the Georgia state line was less than an hour away.

Once we got into Georgia, we stopped at the welcome center to celebrate Ashley and Nicole's first time out of Florida. We got sodas and snacks out of the vending machines, then went out and sat at a picnic table and blended in with all the other travelers.

I taught Ashley and Nicole how to dine and dash at Denny's, steal gas, and make beer runs. I could carry more beer and run faster than they could, so I had them just wait in the car. I also started driving since I was a lot more experienced in traveling and knowing how to read the highway signs without getting lost.

We were getting low on money, so a motel room was definitely out of the question. I sure wanted to have sex with Ashley. All we did up until that point was kiss, and every time we did that, my dick would get so hard, I just wanted to fuck her.

I was beginning to think she was just teasing me the whole time. When we got to a rest area in North Carolina, Ashley went to use the bathroom, and I told Nicole that I thought Ashley was teasing me because she wouldn't even let me touch her body. As soon as I told Nicole that, I got a huge shock that I wasn't expecting. Nicole reached over and started kissing me. My dick got instantly hard, and she grabbed it and said, "I won't tease you." Then we saw Ashley coming out of the restroom, and Nicole told me not to say anything to her.

She didn't have to worry about that. *Hell yeah*. It was on. Nicole was fucking hot. I was definitely gonna try to fuck her that night—some way, somehow.

From that moment on, every chance me and Nicole had, we would kiss and talk, and she didn't have a problem with me feeling all over her sexy-ass body. She loved grabbing my dick through my pants too. *Hell fuckin yeah.* I couldn't wait to give it to her.

We then came up with a plan for later that night. She would tell Ashley that she wanted to ride shotgun for a while. Then when it started to get late, I would tell them I was gonna find a place to sleep because I was getting tired. Ashley could sleep in the backseat, I would sleep in the driver seat, and Nicole would sleep in the passenger seat. That would be perfect because as soon as Ashley passed out in the backseat, me and Nicole would have sex in the passenger seat. That was the best possible plan we could come up with. I give up on Ashley. She wasn't giving shit up. She wouldn't even feel my dick through my pants. I was like, "Let's have some damn fun. We're all on the fucking run." I knew our days were numbered. That's why I wanted to get some pussy before I went to jail. At least I knew Nicole was down for it. I couldn't wait. She was better looking than any girl I had ever had sex with up until that point. I just wanted to pull over and bang her right then and there.

I was also praying to myself, "Dear Lord Jesus, please don't let me get pulled over before tonight. Please let me be able to put my dick inside this sexy ass girl sitting beside me. Please, please, please, Amen."

During that day, we drove all through North Carolina. Wow! What a pretty state. When we got to Virginia, I started getting tired. So much for heading west to California. We had no idea where we were going.

It was also getting late, so I started looking for a place to pull over for the night. I looked in the backseat, and Ashley was out, which I pointed out to Nicole. That's when I really tried to hurry up and find a place to stop. There were no rest areas anywhere around, so I decided the best place to stop would be in a hotel parking lot. I could just blend in with the rest of the cars so me and Nicole could have sex, then we would just crash out for the night. It sounded like the perfect plan.

I stopped at the first hotel I saw, then drove around to the back and found the perfect parking spot in between two other cars.

It was really cold that night, so I left the car running to keep the heat on. I looked back to see if Ashley was still passed out, then reached over to Nicole, and we started kissing.

She unbuttoned my pants, pulled down my zipper, pulled my dick out, and started jacking me off, when all of a sudden, a bright-ass spotlight shined through the back window and scared the shit out of us.

Oh no. Oh, God. Not Now.

I knew it was a cop.

Dammit, Dammit, Dammit, Fuck, Fuck, Fuck.

Did he really have to come right then? I tried to get my pants zipped up and buttoned as fast as I could, while Ashley got a rude awakening.

Well, that was it. We were all going to jail. The cop had already run the tags, and the car had come back stolen because the cop had the spotlight pointed at me, telling me to step out of the car while my dick was still hard. It wouldn't fucking go down, so I stepped out with an obvious hard-on, which I knew he saw. Then another cop pulled up. Dammit, it fucking sucked. I knew I would never see Nicole again.

I didn't even know her phone number or address. Damn, I was so fucking close.

The cop had me sit in the backseat of his car, and I just wanted to start jacking off, thinking of Nicole. Dammit, oh well. I knew I was going to jail, and that's exactly what happened.

I went to an adult jail, and Ashley and Nicole were taken to juvenile hall.

I guess I was lucky I didn't get into more serious trouble because I was eighteen, and they were sixteen and seventeen. I only got charged with escaping from the halfway house.

I was then held in a small local county jail until I could be extradited back to Florida. They also said I would be tried as an adult for escape. I never escaped. I walked away. There were no fences around the halfway house.

I sure thought about Nicole for a long time after that. I never did see her again, but I sure did jack off a lot while I was in jail, thinking of her.

Chapter 58

I stayed in jail for a few weeks, waiting to get extradited back to Florida to face my escape charges and finally be tried as an adult. I was scared to go to a real adult jail. I didn't know what to expect. The jail I was at was really small, and I was in a cell all by myself, but being in a jail in Orlando would be a whole different story. I wasn't looking forward to that.

An extradition service finally came and picked me up. It was a van with about eight other inmates on it, all going to different county jails all over the country. It was the most horrible trip I'd ever taken in my life. I was handcuffed with chains wrapped around my waist, and the handcuffs were hooked to the chains, so I could hardly move my hands. I could barely reach my face, which made it really hard to eat. Because they stopped at fast-food places along the way, for all three meals, it really sucked. My ankles were also shackled.

Trying to sleep was totally out of the question. It was impossible. It was a total nightmare.

I finally arrived at the Orange County Jail in Orlando.

Well, this was it. I made it to the big time. I was really nervous and didn't know what to expect. I went through the whole booking process, which took forever. I went from one ice-cold holding cell to another, and none of them had a mattress or blanket in them. That's all I really cared about at that point. I just wanted to sleep, but I had to wait until the booking process was over before I could even think about doing that, but I still tried. I found a toilet paper roll to use as a pillow and tried to lay down on the ice-cold concrete benches, but that wasn't happening; it was just too dam cold, so I just stayed up and waited until they found a place to house me.

There were about ten other inmates in the holding cell with me who were being really loud and got on my fucking nerves, causing me to suffer more torture.

Two days in a van, all shackled and handcuffed, to a freezing-ass cell for two more fucking days.

What the fuck have I got myself into? All over some pussy that I never even got.

Now I was facing adult escape charges for walking away from a juvenile halfway house. Just fucking lovely.

After the two-day booking process, I was finally given jail clothes and put into a cell that had a mattress. All I wanted to do was sleep, hoping my nightmare would go away.

The first thing I noticed when I was put into my cell was that I was the only white guy among twenty blacks, and boy, they were fucking loud. Jesus Christ. Where the hell had they put me? I'd never seen anything like it.

I asked one of the guys if it was where I would be staying until I went to court, and he said that I would be moving to the main jail downtown in a few days. Thank fucking God, because there was no way in hell I would be able to stay in that cell much longer. It couldn't even think straight, let alone sleep.

Three days of pure hell had passed by when I was finally told I was moving to the main jail downtown. *Yes, get me the fuck out of here.*

When I was brought down there, I was put in a cell with over fifty guys. It was a little better. I found the biggest white guy, who was covered in tattoos, and started talking and hanging out with him. His name was Tank and he was pretty cool. He said I could move into the bunk above his, which was empty, so I did that.

It was loud as fuck in that cell too. Our bunk was right next to the dayroom tables, where all the black inmates played a card game called spades, and they would constantly be slamming the cards on the table.

Tank told me not to say anything to them because they would want to fight me, and it wouldn't be one on one.

I noticed they respected Tank, so I hung out with him, and we played cards together on his bunk, but the constant noise was really irritating me. I didn't want to be in that cell either.

After about three weeks, I just couldn't take it anymore, so I approached the table where four of the loudest guys in the cell were playing spades. I knew I was going against what Tank told me, but I didn't care. I had a plan to get the fuck out of that cell. It was the only thing I could think of to do. So I asked the guys if they could please stop slamming the cards and dominoes on the table. And they said, "Fuck you, Cracker." I was like, "alright," then I went back to my bunk and decided to take a shower. There was no way I could fight them. They were all way bigger than I was. Even one-on-one, the smallest one would kick my ass.

After I finished taking my shower, I walked back to my bunk and noticed all my stuff was all over the floor—my mattress, blankets, everything, and Tank was just sitting there.

"What happened?" I asked. "Who did this?"

Tank just pointed to the spade table and said, "I told you not to say anything to them. "Fuck them motherfuckers."

Then I really knew how to get the fuck out of that cell.

There was a cooler inside the cell that the guards brought to us every morning with coffee in it. Then in the afternoon, they would fill it with Kool-Aid. It was one of those round orange ones with the white lid. I was gonna grab it, then run over to the spade table and start smashing those motherfuckers. But first, I had to wait for the guards to come by the cell so they could save my ass from getting beat up, so I had to wait for them.

Thirty minutes later, I heard the sweet sound of keys coming down the hallway and decided to make my move.

I grabbed the cooler without anyone at the table seeing me, then smashed the first guy on the side of his head. Bam! Perfect shot. Then I got another good swing and hit another guy in his hand when he tried to block the cooler from smashing his face, and that was all I could do before all four of them chased me to the shower and started beating the shit out of me.

It was perfect timing because the guards only saw them jumping me. They never saw me attack them, and my sorry-ass, hardcore, tattooed bunkie didn't do anything to help me.

The guys had me down on the shower floor, beating me, but I was blocking every punch and kick with my arms to protect my face.

All the guards came running in there and saved me, then took me to a single cell all by myself. Perfect. Mission accomplished. Now I could sleep.

One of the guards came to my cell and said I did a good job, that two of the guys had to go to the hospital—one for stitches above his eye and the other one with a broken hand. And I didn't have one mark on me, so I felt good about that. That's what they get for being so disrespectful.

So, that was my first jail experience.

Chapter 59

I called home and asked my mom if there was any way she could help me get out of jail.

She said she would talk to a neighbor of ours who was a lawyer in Orlando and see what he could do. Then, a few days later, he came to the jail to visit me, and I told him what had happened—that I had left the halfway house with two girls. He said he would represent me, but one of his conditions was that I would have to wear a tie. That was easy enough, even though I had never worn a tie or even knew how to put one on. He told me not to worry about it and that he would help me put it on before I saw the judge.

The following week, I went to court looking all sharp in my shirt and tie my lawyer brought for me, and I ended up getting released on probation that day. Damn, I hated probation. But it seemed like I had no other choice. It was a lot better than being in jail, so I accepted the probation and went back home to live with my mom, brothers, and sisters.

My dad was still not around; he was gone for good. I was glad about that because I didn't want to get into it with him again.

I tried my best to do good. I was tired of running and didn't want to go back to jail.

The day after I got home, I went looking for a job. I didn't have a car, so I just went anywhere I could think of that was within walking distance of my house. A guy in our neighborhood had a landscaping company, so I went to see him since I knew how to mow lawns, and he hired me to start the following day, so I was excited about that.

He also had a bad-ass Silverado 4x4 truck that he used to pull his equipment trailer.

My boss must've made good money because he had a house, a brand-new fishing boat, two rottweilers, a bad-ass lifted truck, and a banging-ass wife. Man, I would love to have all those things someday, especially his wife; she was fucking fine as hell. She would sometimes come and help us wearing really tight daisy dukes and tank tops that would show her nipples when she would get all sweaty.

Me and the other coworkers would just drool over her. Our boss was a big-ass country boy, so we didn't dare ever try to hit on her, but I damn sure jacked off a lot thinking of her. I then found out later that she was a stripper at one of the local strip clubs in Fern Park. It was either The House of Babes or Club Juana.

That's probably how my boss was able to afford all his toys.

I worked for him for a while, and my mom must have seen me trying because she said she had a friend who was selling a '77 Cutlass Supreme, and she would see about getting it for me or at least helping me buy it from her for $700. So I ended up buying that, which was the nicest car I've had up until that point. It was green with green interior and had the Oldsmobile 350 rocket motor. It was in mint condition without a scratch on it. I loved it. I was so happy to finally have a car again, which would be a blessing and a curse because I started to remember the yogurt shop in Texas, the shoe store in Vermont, and all the other options that I would have. I wouldn't be limited to just the places around my house, like the apartment complex, golf course, Afcom, sand dunes, or woods. I would be able to branch out and explore new places, especially stores where girls worked.

I couldn't wait to drive all over Orlando and every other city to see what was out there. That's all I thought about.

***

I knew a girl named Michelle who lived a few blocks away from me I had met through Robert.

Since I was back living with my mom and had a car again, I decided to give her a call to see what she was up to. Plus, I was horny and wanted some pussy.

I remember Robert telling me she liked to fuck.

We hit it off pretty good. I told her I was working and had my own car and asked if she wanted to go to the Altamonte Mall and hang out. She was pretty, with long blonde hair and blue eyes, and she did love to fuck.

One night she wanted me to sneak into her bedroom that she shared with her sister, who was a Casselberry cop.

"Hell no, I'm not going over there."

She said it would be OK because her sister worked the midnight shift and would be gone all night. So I went over there, and we were having sex in her bed, which was nice because we were so used to having sex in my car.

When we were finished, we were just kicking back under the covers, completely naked, when all of a sudden, we heard someone coming through the front door of the house.

"Oh shit. Quick, get under the bed; it's my sister."

I didn't even have time to find my underwear and put them on.

"Get my damn clothes for me, and throw them under the bed."

When her sister came into the room, Michelle was in the bed pretending she had just woken up, and I was underneath it, wondering how in the hell I was gonna get outta there.

I was down there listening to them talk and could even see her sister's feet when she started getting undressed. Oh my God, I was trapped under there. I could see my clothes that Michelle shoved under the bed, but I couldn't even move, let alone get dressed, and I didn't see my shoes anywhere.

I then heard her sister saying she was gonna jump in the shower. Yes, it was my chance to get the fuck out of there. As soon as his sister left the room and I heard the shower running, Michelle told me to hurry up and get out of there.

We didn't know her sister was gonna come home early.

I put my underwear on, grabbed my clothes, and Michelle told me to get dressed outside.

I only found one of my shoes, so I threw my clothes and one shoe out the window, climbed out, and got dressed. I couldn't believe I left with only one shoe. Oh well, at least I didn't get caught.

I then walked home with one shoe on. Well, that was exciting. It was also my last time sneaking over there. I didn't want to be anywhere near a cop, especially a Casselberry one. I had a bad experience with one of them.

One night, Michelle told me she was gonna take her mom's car while her mom was asleep and asked if I wanted to go drinking with her. Then she would bring the car back before her mom woke up.

That sounded like fun. She wanted to drive her mom's car because it was brand new, so

she picked me up around midnight, then we went to the store to find someone to buy us some beer. Back then, it was real easy. All we had to do was park right in front of the store, then when we saw someone who was over twenty-one and looked cool, Michelle would call them to the car and ask them if they could buy her a 12-pack, and they always would for her.

Afcom was the perfect place to park because it was dark and secluded late at night after they closed, so we went there, sat in the car, listened to music, got drunk, got naked, then fucked until 4 a.m. before we decided that she needed to get the car back before her mom woke up.

We had a lot of fun together, and the sex was great. But there was one thing I really hated about her. She spent too much damn time doing her hair and makeup. It took her over two hours to get ready every day. Her hair had to be perfect. Not one single hair could be out of place. It was insane. The very first fight we ever had was over her fucking hair.

One weekend, we were on our way to Daytona in my car, having a great time, when all of a sudden, she said, "I have to go home."

"Why?"

"My hair is not acting right; it's messed up, and I have to go home and fix it."

"Are you fucking serious? You look fine."

She then got all moody and pissed, all because her hair wasn't acting right. I got so mad, I turned around and took her all the way back to Winter Springs and dropped her off at her house.

After that day, I didn't care too much for her, and we drifted apart.

All because of her, I can't stand a woman that wears a ton of makeup and takes forever to get ready. I love a naturally beautiful woman who can wake up in the morning, throw a baseball cap on, with no makeup, and be ready to go. Now that's beauty. That's what I want.

I had much better things to do, like finding places to flash.

I was still at my landscaping job, but as soon as I would get off work, and especially on my days off, I would drive all over Seminole and Orange Counties looking for stores where women worked or anywhere else girls would be.

One day I was driving down Highway 436 toward Altamonte Springs to see what I could find. I kept driving past the Altamonte Mall, just looking for certain types of stores, when I noticed a strip mall on my left that had a store called Clothestime. Now that sounded like a store where women would shop, so I pulled in to check it out.

I was cruising through the parking lot really slow, checking out all the stores, when I saw a really hot chick walking across the parking lot, then going into Clothestime.

That's when I started getting really excited, and the first thing that came to my mind was I had to hide my car; there was no way I could let anyone see me and it. I needed to check things out on foot.

There was a restaurant next door that had a really big parking lot that was out of view from the strip mall, so I parked there, then walked back over to the Clothestime to have a look.

It was a woman's clothing store, and it was also in the perfect location. It was the last store at one end of the strip mall, which was perfect for what I had in mind.

I learned that one of the most important things about being a good flasher was location, location, location. Every place I flashed had to be perfect. That was because I needed a good getaway. That was the most important part because the most terrifying thing that could ever possibly happen to me would be getting caught. I didn't even want to think about that. I didn't know what I would ever do if that happened, so I always made sure that I had a good getaway.

I couldn't just walk up to a girl and flash her at the spur of the moment. I needed to plan each incident very carefully. The reason I favored the stores on the ends of strip malls was because I would be able to flash, then take off running along the side of the building, then around the back to wherever I hid my car. It was a lot harder to flash a girl in front of a store that was in the middle of a strip mall because there would usually be too much foot traffic on both sides, which would attract a lot of attention to myself trying to get away, especially if the girl started screaming and yelling. So, I learned that the end stores were a lot safer because I could flash, then be out of sight pretty quick by running along the side of the store toward the back without attracting a lot of attention.

I also noticed something very nice. The restaurant next to the Clothestime was in a totally separate building, and in between the two buildings was a really narrow alleyway that led to the back of the mall and restaurant.

It was the perfect setup because the front doors of the Clothestime were right next to the alley. *Wow!* Talk about the perfect getaway. I was in heaven because all I had to do was stand right by the front doors of the Clothestime and wait for a girl to come in or out, flash her, then take off through the alley, run across the back parking lot of the restaurant, then to my car.

It was the perfect setup. *Hell yeah.* I had found a new spot.

My heart was racing so fast; the anticipation was driving me crazy; I couldn't believe it.

I then walked back to my car to make sure it was in a good spot. My adrenaline was really pumping because I knew I was gonna flash a girl that day no matter what. I would also get to choose whatever girl I wanted. *Wow!* It was the greatest feeling in the world for me. I had found my drug of choice.

I walked back over to the front of the Clothestime and waited. I had a good view of the parking lot, so I could see when a girl pulled up. I also decided it would be better if I flashed a girl coming into the store. I would rather them run into the store than out into the parking lot screaming. I also didn't need them running back to their cars, then driving over to where I had my car parked, and see me get into it. That wouldn't be good either. I would much rather have them run into the store, so I could make a nice, safe, clean getaway.

As I was standing there, I saw two women walk out of the store.

I also learned that if I was gonna flash, I was gonna make it worth my while. I just wasn't gonna flash any girl. She had to be fucking fine, with a nice body. The type I knew wouldn't give me the time of day. Those were the ones I wanted to flash, like the girls I saw in Playboy.

I have set my standards very high, so I would stand out there all day if I had to. I didn't care. I was gonna show my big hard dick to a fine-ass girl.

A couple more girls came out, but they weren't up to my standards.

The one thing I didn't like was that I couldn't stand there and jack off with lotion like I wanted, which really sucked. All I could do was stand there with my hands in my pocket and play with myself that way until the right girl came along. I would have to come up with something, so I could jack off with lotion while waiting.

I was still too scared to walk into stores and flash, but as I said before, I would definitely build up to that.

I also had to try and disguise myself as best I could, just in case. So what I came up with was, as soon as I saw a girl get out of her car that I was gonna flash, I would run into the alley really quick, take my T-shirt off, put it on my head, pull my pants down to the middle of my thighs, then walk right up next to the front door while they were walking in. That was the plan. Then, finally, after about two hours of waiting, I got my wish.

Two blondes in a red Honda pulled up. Hell yeah, there was a God. They were both around nineteen and had nice bodies. *Oh my fucking God.*

They were giggling and laughing as they got out of their car.

I ran into the alley, pulled my shirt off, saying to myself, *You won't be laughing in about thirty seconds.*

I then pulled my pants and underwear down and said, "Here goes nothing." I never had a problem with my dick staying hard, so I was always fully hard every time I flashed a girl. I also loved the thought of getting two or more girls at once, which made it even more thrilling.

I walked out to the front of the store and started waving my dick at them, asking if they wanted to suck it. That's when one of them yelled, "YOU FUCKING PERVERT," as they both rushed into the store.

I then ran back into the alley, pulled my pants up, put my T-shirt on, and got the fuck out of there as fast as I could, running back to my car with my adrenaline pumping and my heart about to beat out of my chest. *Hell fuckin yeah.* That was perfect, and they were both fine as hell. "Yeah, I'm a fucking pervert, the world's greatest pervert at that. I have the plaque to prove it." Wow! That was a great day. I couldn't wait to do it again. But I would definitely have to wait a few days before going back there.

That was my first experience with a Clothestime and wouldn't be my last. It would become one of my favorite places to flash. So, if you ever got flashed, in or outside of a Clothestime, I'm sure that was me.

Chapter 60

When a person lives heedlessly, his craving grows like a
creeping vine.
He runs now here and now there, as if looking for fruit;
a monkey in the forest
~ Dhammapada 334

I was driving around looking for places to flash, which was very thrilling for me. I guess you could say the thrill of the hunt; I enjoyed searching for new places because the more places I found, the more places I could flash. Work was pretty slow at my landscaping job. I was only working three days a week; then, eventually, my boss just let me go altogether. It was the slow season, and there just wasn't enough work.

I was actually glad in a way because now I had a lot more free time to drive around and look for places to flash.

I remembered those girls from Rollins College who I flashed at the golf course, and it gave me a great idea. I could drive out to the local colleges and see what I could there. The University of Central Florida was really close to where I went to high school in Oviedo, so I would definitely check that out first.

At least I didn't have to worry about going to work any longer, so I was free to go anywhere I wanted. Why would I want to be out mowing lawns when I could be out flashing and jacking off in front of pretty girls?

I got up early one morning and waited for my brothers and sisters to go to school and my mom to go to work, then took off to the UCF campus with a big bottle of lotion just in case. Man, I was so excited. I had the whole day to look for girls. It didn't get much better than that.

When I got to the campus, I started cruising through the parking lots. My God, there was pussy everywhere, and my dick started getting hard. How in the hell was I gonna flash?

I couldn't do it in my car. That would be fucking stupid.

I was parked in a parking lot just watching girls walk by my car, so I pulled my Dickout, put some lotion on it, and started jacking off, making sure no one could see me; I was just sitting there watching all the pretty girls walk by. I needed to flash them somehow.

I didn't want to sit in my car all day and jack off without flashing. That wouldn't be fun, so I put my dick away and started driving around again, then decided to leave because it was just too hard and risky to flash there.

As I was leaving, I noticed some woods to my left and a walking trail that ran along them, running from the college to the main entrance of the campus, and that's where I saw a really pretty blond wearing a pink backpack walking on that trail. Yes, I had a plan, but I needed to hide my fucking car somewhere.

I continued driving down the street toward the main entrance. I needed to hide my car, then come back and walk down that trail on foot to check out.

I saw an apartment complex on my right and pulled in there, parked, then walked back toward the trail. That's when I saw more girls using that trail to get to and from the college. *Wow!* I was in heaven. I couldn't believe it. There were also a few guys using the trail, so I had to be careful of them. I didn't need to be getting chased.

I was walking on the trail toward the college. The woods were on my right and the street on my left. Girls and guys were walking and riding bikes past me in both directions.

Then halfway down the trail, I found exactly what I was looking for—a hiding spot in the woods next to the trail, right behind a bunch of bushes. It was fucking perfect.

When the coast was clear, I got off the trail and went behind those bushes to see what kind of vantage point I would have from there.

I couldn't have found a better spot. I could see who was coming up and down the trail in both directions without them seeing me. I even hid there and watched a couple of girls walk by while my heart was racing big time. I couldn't believe I had found the most perfect spot in the world; it was meant to be. It was way better than the woods behind my house or the golf course.

What made it so great was that college girls were guaranteed to walk by all day, every day, and I could pick and choose whichever ones I wanted to flash, and it wasn't a real busy trail, which made it even better. I would see a girl walk by, all by herself, about every fifteen minutes, then there would be a little rush of girls and guys walking together, but it was mostly girls walking by themselves. I was in fuckin' heaven.

I needed to get back to my car and come up with a good getaway plan; my car was just too far away. But it was the only place I could park it.

The woods across the street from the apartments were the same woods that the trail ran next to, so I decided that after I exposed myself, I would run deeper into the woods and come out right across the street from the apartment complex. The riskiest part would be running across Alafaya Trail, which was a really busy road. My best bet would be to flash girls on their way to the campus. That way, when they took off running, they would hopefully run toward the campus and not in the direction that I needed to run because that would be all bad. I always wanted girls to run in the opposite direction that I had to run. So as I was cumming, I wanted them going.

I grabbed my lotion and headed back to the bushes. As I was walking down the trail, I saw a couple more blondes. *Wow!* Only if they knew what I was getting ready to do. Another reason I loved the spot was that I could take off all my clothes, which made it even better.

I loved being completely naked out in the woods. Plus, it gave the girls a greater shock to see me completely naked, standing in front of them, jacking off. It was also more of an adrenaline rush for me.

I got behind the bushes, took all my clothes off, put my T-shirt on my head, and started jacking off with my lotion while watching up and down the trail. It was so thrilling. Just the waiting and anticipation was the greatest feeling ever. I could stay behind those bushes all day, just knowing I could flash any girl I wanted at any moment. It was an incredible feeling.

I was also being very picky. My thinking was if I was gonna flash, I might as well make it worth my while and wait for a super-hot chick, which wouldn't take long because it seemed like every girl that walked by was fucking fine. It was just a matter of catching one all by herself without any guys anywhere near her.

I was there for six hours when I finally decided it was time. I could have gotten several during that time, but I just enjoyed the feeling of being out there.

I saw a long blonde ponytail swinging from side to side. Hell yeah. I loved blondes, especially natural ones, and one was coming right to me as I was praying nobody else would come by at the same time. It would only take her a minute to reach me. As long as no guys came by within that time, I would be fine. I didn't ask for much. She was 30 seconds away, so I put some more lotion on, 15 seconds, 10, 9, 8, 7, 6, 5. I walked out on the trail right in front of her ... 4, 3, 2 ... she saw me and froze ... 1 ... blastoff. I started cumming right as she was staring at my dick. She was watching it all shoot out with her beautiful green eyes. Then she said, "That's fucking disgusting."

I ran back to the bushes, grabbed my clothes, and took off running as fast as I could into the woods while trying to put my clothes on at the same time. Damn, it was a long way to my car. Thank God nobody was chasing me.

Wow! That was great. I loved it when girls stuck around for those few extra seconds and watched me cum. It didn't get any better than that. Most girls take off running and screaming. But the ones who freeze up and watch me like that. I love them. *Hell, fuckin' yeah.*

From that day on, I was fucking hooked on that spot and went there every day, not even thinking about the girls calling the cops. Well, I did kinda think about it, but I just didn't care. I wasn't giving up that spot. Plus, I knew I had a good getaway. If a cop car did come, I would see it long before it saw me. Then I would just run deeper into the woods until it passed by.

But that never happened. I went there every day for at least six hours a day for over a month and flashed over forty girls. I don't know how many actually called cops, but I never did see one go by.

I finally came to my senses and knew I was pushing my luck, so I decided to take a break from there. Plus, my money was running out. I needed to find another job. It took a lot of gas to do all the driving I did. *Wow!* What a great spot. It was the best spot I've ever found, and I would definitely be back.

Instead of driving around looking for girls to flash, I went driving around looking for a job.

The one thing I didn't like was being broke. I couldn't drive around looking for girls to flash without gas, so a job was my number-one priority for the moment because I was down to my last tank of gas, so I needed a job pretty bad.

I looked in the yellow pages for landscaping and lawn maintenance companies, copied down all the addresses, then drove to all the ones that were fairly close to apply. Lawn maintenance was the only thing that I really knew how to do at the time, plus I enjoyed working outside.

I went to three different places and got lucky at the third one. They hired me on the spot and said I could start the following day, to be there at 6 a.m.

It was a really big company. That had six trucks and trailers, loaded down with equipment with three guys to a truck.

The only thing I didn't like about that job, and every other job I've had, was I hated waiting two weeks to get my first paycheck. I hated that shit. Two weeks was an eternity for me.

***

As I was driving home one day, I noticed that a girl around my age moved into a house right down the street from me on Lombardy Road who was fucking hot. I saw her out in front of her house when I drove by. I was definitely gonna have to stop and talk to her the next time I saw her out there.

I also saw a beautiful, white '76 Corvette in her driveway. Man, I would love to have one of those too.

After that day, I made sure I drove by her house at least ten times a day, hoping she didn't have a boyfriend.

It took me a few days before I saw her again, and that's when I pulled into her driveway and started talking to her. *Wow!* She was even prettier up close. Her name was Rhonda. She had beautiful green eyes, blonde hair, and a perfect body. Just my type. She was seventeen and didn't have a boyfriend, so we ended up talking for over two hours in her driveway.

The corvette was her mom's, and her stepdad had a really nice Ford Bronco. Rhonda didn't have a car. We hit it off pretty good. She liked to drink and smoke cigarettes, and I definitely had to put my flashing on hold because she was beautiful and would be, by far, the hottest girl I'd ever had sex with.

We exchanged numbers and talked every day. Her stepdad was really strict, so she would have to wait until both he and her mom were at work before inviting me over.

We would then hang out in her room, listen to music, and drink beer.

After our first few beers together, we became boyfriend and girlfriend. *Hell yeah.* Cheers, we tapped our cans together.

The very first time we had sex, she wanted to do it in the living room because her bedroom was all the way in the back of the house, and she wanted to be able to hear if her mom or dad came home. That way, I could run to her room and jump out her window. I would also leave my car at my house because she wasn't allowed to have anyone in the house when her parents were gone. So we grabbed a blanket off her bed, brought it to the living room, and spread it out on the floor.

The first time having sex with a girl was always fun and exciting because I never knew what to expect. I couldn't wait to see Rhonda's body. She had perfect tits, perfect ass, perfect everything, and she was pretty.

The thing that scared me the most about having sex with a girl for the first time was cumming too fast. *Please, Lord. Don't let that happen.*

We started off kissing, then she let me take her shirt off, then her bra, then her jeans and panties.

Oh my fucking God. Her body was perfect. She had a body just like the girls in Playboy. She could definitely pose in any of those magazines for sure. She even had that bikini tan line that I love so much. Damn, she was hot. Then she said, "What are you waiting for? Take your clothes off."

She didn't have to ask me twice; my clothes were off within seconds.

She then told me to lay down on my back, and she went straight to my hard Dick and started sucking it. Yes, I was in love. What really drove me crazy was when she would look up at me with her beautiful green eyes while my Dick was in her mouth. She would stop to ask me if I liked it and if she was doing OK. Hell yeah, I liked it. I liked it so much, I had to make her stop before I came all over her pretty face, which I really wanted to do, but miraculously I held back before that happened. I wanted to put my Dick inside her pretty blond pussy, but first I went down and licked and sucked on it until she couldn't take it any longer, and she started begging me to fuck her, saying, "Please fuck me, please fuck me, please fuck me with your big hard dick."

Wow! It was the best pussy I ever had.

The best memory I have of her, besides her beautiful green eyes looking up at me with a mouthful of dick, was when we finished having sex, she would always get up and go into the bathroom, and I would always stare at her perfect ass as she walked away, with their little bikini tan line. She had the nicest ass I had ever seen, and it was all mine. *Hell yeah.* I was in love; she had me hooked.

We had sex every chance we got. I would even sneak over to her house in the middle of the night and climb through her bedroom window when her parents were asleep. Then, of course, during the week, when her parents were at work.

Sneaking over in the middle of the night lasted a while, until one day, her dad was out doing yard work and saw all my footprints in the dirt outside her window, and put two and two together, then screwed her screen shut. I thought about bringing a screwdriver over there with me but decided I better not. He was probably gonna pay more attention from then on, so we just settled on the weekdays. We had a lot more time that way anyway and didn't have to be as quiet. Plus, I liked seeing her body during the day.

Rhonda's mom seemed to like me, but her dad obviously didn't. I don't know why; maybe it was the little yellow diamond shape sign that I had on my car window that said, "Don't laugh, your daughter may be in here." Who knows?

Me and Rhonda found that sign in Spencer's at the mall.

After a couple of months of dating Rhonda, she called me up and said she might be pregnant because she hadn't started her period. She even told her mom and dad, and that was when all hell broke loose. Her dad was pissed and wanted me to come over so he and her mom could talk to me.

Oh shit, here we go.

So I went over there, and they sat me down at the kitchen table, then gave me a big long speech about Rhonda's and my age, and how would we be able to take care of a baby, and all that.

Her mom asked me what I planned on doing if Rhonda was pregnant. I said what any eighteen-year-old would've said. I would take care of it and do whatever it took, knowing damn well I wasn't ready for a kid. I couldn't even take care of myself, let alone a baby.

What got me the most upset was Rhonda wasn't even pregnant. She had her period a couple of days later, so I had to go through all that abuse from her parents for nothing—not only verbal abuse but I also got physically attacked by her father the following day

I was driving by Rhonda's house on my way to the Circle K and was stopped at the stop sign on the corner of Lombardy and Edgemon when I saw her dad out in their front yard. As soon as he saw me, he ran to his Bronco to come after me.

What the fuck did he want?

I was halfway to the Circle K when he got behind me and started flashing his lights, wanting me to stop. So I pulled into the bank that was on the corner of Edgemon and Highway 434 and stopped by the drive-through teller lanes.

He then pulled up behind me, jumped out of his truck, came right up to my open window, punched me in my face, and told me to stay the fuck away from his daughter.

I couldn't believe he actually hit me. I was only 150 lbs., if that, and he was a grown man over 200 lbs. There was no way I could fight him. I wouldn't have a chance. So, I just drove home and didn't say anything to my mom or anybody. I wished I had a dad I could tell, or someone bigger that would have stuck up for me and gone over there and punched him in his face.

But I didn't have anyone like that. Rhonda couldn't believe it when I told her.

"See what you started? All for nothing. You weren't even pregnant. Now let's go fuck. I might as well get you pregnant since I'm being accused of it."

I couldn't even park in her driveway and talk to her anymore. Just like every other girlfriend I've had, I had to sneak to do everything. I hated that shit.

It was mainly just her dad. Her mom was still cool with me, so I had to hide from him.

Why couldn't all my girlfriends' parents be like my mom? My mom didn't care who my girlfriends were. Well, except one. She hated Christine, which I'm sure was because she was over eighteen at the time, and I was still a minor. But, oh well, having girlfriends' parents hate me was just something I was gonna have to get used to.

Chapter 61

It is a man's own mind, not his enemy or foe,
That lures him into evil ways.
~ The teachings of Buddha

I was at work one morning talking to the guys on my crew, and they were telling me that we had a new contract at a big apartment complex in Orlando. That was cool. I had experience at apartment complexes, and it had nothing to do with mowing or landscaping them, so I was eager to get there and scope things out for other reasons.

We arrived there at 7 a.m. The complex was so big that we would spend the entire day there.

Our first step was to cut the grass, so I grabbed a mower and started cutting around the front entrance.

While I was cutting, I saw a girl walking by who was around sixteen and probably a high school student because she had a backpack slung over her shoulder. *Wow!* She was fine.

Then she stopped on the curb by the front entrance of the complex and just sat down. I looked at my watch and memorized the time. She was obviously waiting for her school bus.

I tried to shield my face from her because I was already making plans. I kept mowing but kept a safe distance away while keeping an eye on her to make sure she was really waiting on a bus.

And sure enough, about ten minutes later, a bus stopped and picked her up. *Hell yeah.* The moment I saw that I knew I was gonna flash her. But how? That was the question.

Talk about a trigger. From that moment, my addiction kicked in and took over.

She was constantly on my mind all day; I couldn't even concentrate on working.

I asked a guy on my crew if we would be there again the following day, and he said yes, which was great because I needed to see if she walked to that bus stop at the same time and if so, I made up my mind. I was definitely quitting that job. Flashing her was more important than a job. Plus, I couldn't flash her, then a week later, she sees me working there. That would be a for-sure bust. I wasn't gonna be that stupid. I was definitely gonna quit, but first, I had to see if she went there every morning and if so, it was on.

What got me really excited was right behind where she sat on the curb was a row of bushes that would provide me with the perfect place to hide. I could even get completely naked behind them. *Hell yeah.* I could walk right up next to her, completely naked. Yeah, that would really shock her. Man, I couldn't fucking wait. *Fuck yeah. Hell, fuckin' yeah.*

The following morning, we were back at the apartment complex, and sure enough, the girl sat on the curb at the same time to wait on her bus. My adrenaline was really pumping, just knowing it was my last day at work, then I would be able to show her my dick and jack off in front of her. It didn't get any more exciting than that. It's what I lived for.

I was supposed to get paid four days later, but I couldn't even wait for that. I had to flash her the following day no matter what. Nothing could stop me. I also made sure the company wasn't gonna be there that day, which was very important. I couldn't let any of the guys see me there the day after I quit. Man, I was so excited, just knowing what I was gonna do.

I got home that night and didn't tell my mom I quit. My plan was to get up and pretend I was going to work the following morning like always, but instead, I would go straight to that complex and find a good place to hide my car. I also wanted to give myself plenty of time. I wanted to be in those bushes at least an hour early. The anticipation was unbelievable.

I wanted to get there early to make sure I was all lotioned up and as hard as I could be, which was never a problem, but I just wanted to be ready and didn't want to have to rush anything.

I woke up the following morning, made sure I had my bottle of lotion, then headed out the door, pretending I was going to work. What a wonderful day it was gonna be.

I got to the apartment complex in plenty of time and decided the best place to hide my car would be in the back, mixed with all the other cars.

The bus stop was out front, so all I would have to do was flash her, put my clothes on really fast, which was always the hard part when I was completely naked because I had to get dressed before I could take off running, and when girls took off screaming, it made it even harder to put my clothes on because I never knew if someone would be chasing me or not, so I needed to get dressed really fast and get the fuck out of there as quick as possible.

I would later get the nickname Flash Gordon because I would be gone in a flash.

Trust me. Girls might be running away from me screaming, but I was more scared of them than they were of me. They just didn't know that.

I would then run through the apartments to my car and drive out the back entrance. It would be an easy getaway.

Another thing I would always do when I flashed and didn't want the girls running in the same direction, I needed to run was I would approach them on the side I didn't want them running. Like in this case, when she sat on the curb, the apartments were to her left, so that's the side I would approach her from. That way, I could block her from running toward the apartments. Their natural instinct was to run away from me, not toward me. We can't be running in the same direction. That would be all bad.

I parked in a great spot, grabbed my lotion, and headed for the bushes with my adrenaline pumping and my heart racing big time. God, I was so fucking excited.

My dick was hard before I even got to the bushes without even touching it.

When I got to the front of the apartments, I looked around to make sure nobody saw me, then ducked behind the bushes. *Wow!* What a perfect spot.

I knew it would be just a one-time deal, so I needed to make it worth my while because I wasn't coming back. *So, get ready, baby; you're getting ready to get the surprise of your life.*

I had about forty-five minutes before she got there, so I took off all my clothes and got ready. I didn't even bother putting my T-shirt on my head. I figured I was so far away from Winter Springs and didn't plan on coming back, so why bother? I started jacking off nice and slow with the lotion, making sure I didn't cum. I kept getting close but would always stop myself. I needed to save it for her. I must have stopped myself six times when I looked at my watch and saw that she would be there any minute. I put more lotion on, looked through the bushes, and sure enough, she was coming. My heart was really racing as I was thinking, *I'm fucking nuts; who does this kinda thing?* Oh well. Nothing could stop me. She walked by looking sexy as ever, with her long brown hair. *All right. Go sit down like a good girl. Yes, perfect, here I come.*

I made sure the coast was clear before walking out to her. She didn't even see me right away because she was writing something in a notebook. I got right next to her and said, "Excuse me."

Her eyes got really huge when she saw my hard-on. "Will you suck this for me?" She then jumped up really fast, saying, "What the fuck are you doing? What's your problem?"

That's when I saw a car turning into the complex, and I ran like hell back to the bushes before the driver saw me. I didn't even have a chance to cum. That car really fucked me up.

I got dressed as fast as possible and got the fuck out of there.

The girl took off walking in the opposite direction like I had hoped and thank God the driver of the car didn't see me. I then ran all way back to my car. *Wow!* What an adrenaline rush that was, especially after a clean getaway. Hell yeah, that would be something she would never forget.

How did you like that big hard dick, baby? Go tell all your high school friends about that.

Since I didn't get the chance to cum, I was still horny as hell, and it was only eight o'clock in the morning, and I knew exactly where I was gonna go: UCF, here I come. Then I would head over to Clothestime and flash some more. Yes, it was gonna be a great day.

I went to UCF and flashed three girls at once, then went to Clothestime and got two more. What a great day, and I could've been at work mowing lawns. Why the fuck would I want to be mowing lawns when I could be jacking off in front of high school and college girls? *Wow!* What an addiction it was turning out to be. It was gonna take over my life; I could already see it happening. There wasn't anything more important or exciting. It's all I wanted to do; nothing else mattered.

Chapter 62

Now that I was out of a job, I had a lot of free time on my hands that I enjoyed very much. I also had a little spending money, so I figured, what the hell, I was gonna do some partying.

I decided to go see my old friend Mike, who lived in the trailer park by the sand dunes, and see what he was up to. I hadn't seen him in a while, and a little coke sounded good right about then, so I stopped by his house to see if he was home. Sure enough, he still lived there, so we went to the store and bought a case of Budweiser.

It was 3 o'clock when we started drinking in his trailer, he then called his coke connection, and that's when the party really started. A few more of his friends came over, and we were having a great time, listening to Creedence Clearwater Revival, the Eagles, Bob Seger, and Pink Floyd. We were just jamming out and snorting lines. We finished off the case, did another beer run, and we're getting pretty buzzed.

I didn't think I was gonna make it home that night. I was getting fucked up.

It was getting late, and Mike's other friends all took off, so Mike and I decided to see what was going on around Winter Springs. What a great idea. Let's go drive around drunk.

They weren't as hard on drunk drivers back then, at least not that I was aware of. It seemed like everyone was doing it. I even saw my dad doing it a few times, so I really didn't think too much of it; it was just the thing to do.

We were just cruising around, getting low on beer again, so we decided to stop at the ABC Liquor before all the stores stopped selling it. But instead of getting more beer, we got some Mad Dog 20/20 grape wine. Yeah, that sounded good. Now we would have Budweiser, cocaine, and Mad Dog running through our veins.

We continued cruising while passing the bottle back and forth. We were really getting smashed. We went to the Circle K in Winter Springs to see what was going on over there. We parked on the side by the pay phones just to kick back in the car and pretend we were using the phone and watch all the people going in and out of the store to see if we could see anybody we knew. It was also kind of a hangout, where people would meet up, talk, and bullshit with each other.

We were there for up thirty minutes when a kid named Allen from my neighborhood pulled up right next to me in his blue '76 Firebird. I was checking out his car, and we started talking. I asked him what kind of motor he had in it and if it was fast. He then told me that he could beat me in a race.

"I don't think so." I told him I had a 350 rocket motor in my car, and I would blow him away.

"Come on. Let's go. Where do you want to race?"

For some reason, I said, "Let's go to Murphy Road," which was a terrible road for a drag race. It was all residential with a lot of curves, but we took off and headed in that direction.

We took Edgemon down to Murphy, took a right, then we pulled right up next to each other and came to a stop.

We both had passengers. I had Mike, and Allen had a friend of his who stuck his arm out the window and counted to three, threw his arm down, and we took off. I immediately took the lead.

We were supposed to race to a small bridge that was about five blocks away, the same bridge where I got my first kiss from Cindy.

We were hauling ass. I was doing over 100 mph when I crossed that bridge and blew his ass away. The speed limit was maybe 35 mph at the most. But I just wanted to show off and kept going even faster. Then the last words I heard Mike say to me were, "Slow down, man." Then a curve came up, and I lost control.

All I remembered after Mike told me to slow down was metal crunching, glass shattering, tires squealing, flipping over and over, more glass shattering, more metal crunching. It just seemed to go on forever. I had no control over the car at all.

Finally, everything stopped. I remember being upside down, and Mike was squished in the seat next to me.

"Mike, are you OK?" I looked over at him, and he was covered in blood, not answering me. *Oh my God.* He was dead. He wasn't even moving. *Oh my God, I just killed him.*

"Mike, wake up." I started shaking him, and he wouldn't even move. Then I heard someone trying to talk to me through my window, asking me if I was OK. They told me not to move and that an ambulance was on its way. I told them I couldn't move anyway. I was stuck, and the steering wheel was pushing against my legs.

"I think my friend is dead." I then asked them if they could get me something to drink because I thought I was gonna pass out.

My face was also bleeding, and my ribs were hurting really bad. The person handed me a Big Gulp cup full of ice and soda, which made me feel better.

I could hear the sirens coming from miles away, and when the ambulance arrived, I told them to get my friend out first.

The Fire Department also came and had to cut us both out of the car.

There were two ambulances, one for me and one for Mike. There were fire trucks and police cars everywhere. I saw them putting yellow tape around the scene. *Oh God, please don't let Mike be dead. This can't be happening.*

They loaded me up in the ambulance and took me to South Seminole Community Hospital in Longwood. I was in a lot of pain. I couldn't even sit up by myself, and my left eye was split open. But all I cared about and wanted to know was if Mike was OK.

Every doctor and nurse I saw, that's all I would ask them until finally, I got an answer.

Yes, Mike would be fine. He just got knocked uncon-scious. *Whew, thank God.*

I would also be OK. I just had a few broken ribs and a cut above my left eye. I was released from the hospital later that morning. I never knew the extent of Mike's injuries, but he had to stay in the hospital a lot longer, and I never talked to or saw him again.

I didn't realize how lucky I was until I saw how horrific the accident was the following day.

I had a brace around my waist for my broken ribs and stitches over my left eye, and I could barely get in and out of bed. But I really wanted to check out the crash site just to see what happened and how much damage I did.

So I walked over to Murphy Road, but first, I stopped at Rhonda's and asked if she wanted to go with me. Rhonda hugged me and said she was glad I was OK. She said she heard all the sirens, then found out I had been in an accident. She was so worried about me, so we walked over there together, holding hands.

I showed her where we started racing; then, we walked down Murphy Road until we saw the skid marks. *Wow!* We continued to follow them, trying to figure them out. We saw them plow through three mailboxes, three yards, three cars, and finally ending up in a house that was heavily damaged.

Oh my God. I was so lucky the people living there were asleep and not watching TV in their living room because that is where I ended up.

From the moment the crash started, Rhonda started finding all kinds of little parts and pieces that had broken off my car. We couldn't figure out what they were, but she kept them all.

She even found a bumper sticker that I had on my back window, with glass all stuck to the back of it. She also found the little sign that said, "Don't laugh; your daughter may be in here."

She kept all that stuff on a shelf in her bedroom, her little souvenirs of me almost killing myself.

If that crash scene didn't scare me, I sure was gonna get scared when I saw my car.

In fact, I got so scared when I saw my car that I would never drink and drive again.

I was lucky to even be alive.

I found out where my car got towed. I had to see if it could be fixed, and I needed to get my stuff out of it. The towing company was actually on the same street that Afcom was on, behind my house, so me and Rhonda walked over there and asked them how I could get my car back. That's when they looked at me and said, "You're still alive? You're the luckiest kid we know." Then they said, "You don't want it back. There's nothing left of it." Then they let me go back and look at it. *Holy shit.* A '77 Cutlass isn't a small car, and when I saw it, I couldn't believe my eyes. You couldn't even tell what kind of car it was. It was a miracle I was alive.

Rhonda started crying. She even knew I was lucky to be alive. She didn't realize how bad it really was until she saw it. I didn't even know how bad it was. There wasn't one single piece on that car that was reusable. It was 100 percent totaled.

While I was looking inside it for spare change, cassette tapes or whatever else I could find, I couldn't believe my eyes when I saw two things. One was a fucking mailbox, and two, the roof on the passenger side was totally smashed down into the passenger seat.

Now I knew why Mike was so close to me. He was forced over to my side, and that's why my right ribs were broken. We were not wearing seat belts, which I know for a fact saved Mike's life because if he had one on, he wouldn't have been able to slide over toward me, and he would've been crushed to death by the roof.

I also saw a lot of beer cans. That's another thing I couldn't believe. I never got charged with DUI, which was really weird.

The only thing I could think of was one of the Winter Springs cops that was first on the scene must have known who I was and knew my mom from her store. Because it was an obvious case of drunk driving that I never got charged with.

A few weeks later, I got a call from an attorney who was representing the people whose house I crashed into. I think I caused around $60,000 in damage to the house.

The lawyer asked me if I owned anything. I told him that I had a Curtis Mathis stereo in my bedroom. That was it. He then told me I was lucky because he couldn't squeeze blood from a turnip, then hung up on me.

So that was my brush with death. It was definitely a wake-up call. Even to this day, I will never drink and drive. It really scared me. I can't even be a passenger in a car if I know the driver has been drinking. I can't even be a passenger if someone is speeding. That's how much that accident affected me.

I still remember the moment I lost control at over 100 mph. It was like the ground was covered in oil, and there was nothing I could do to save it. All I could do was close my eyes and pray.

So, whoever is reading this, especially teenagers who think it's cool to drink and drive, then go out and race people. It's not cool because, in a split second, you can be dead, and all the passengers in your car will be dead too, or even worse, you survive, and all your passengers die.

How would you like to live with that for the rest of your life?

I am extremely lucky to be alive and live to tell you about it. Drunk driving is not cool. If you drink and drive, you're a fucking idiot.

Chapter 63

When overspread by extreme vice-
Like a sal tree by a vine-
You do to yourself
What an enemy would wish.
Dhammapada 162

Later in my life, people would ask me, "Why do you flash women? You're a good-looking guy. You could get any girl you want." But they just didn't understand my addiction.

I've had beautiful girlfriends. I had Rhonda, who had a banging-ass body, and was beautiful.

I could've been at her house fucking her, but it just wasn't the same as being in an apartment complex laundry room, jacking off, waiting for some pretty, unsuspecting girl to do her laundry, lay out by the pool, or work out in the weight room, or any girl to come along so I could completely shock her. It was a lot more exciting than having sex. Just seeing the shocked look on their faces was such an adrenaline rush for me. I fuckin' loved it.

I spent the whole weekend at an apartment complex and really pushed my luck because, on Saturday, I flashed two girls there, then came back on Sunday and flashed three more.

I was really getting bold, thinking I was uncatchable, but I knew I was just lucky. I had been flashing for five years and had yet to be caught. I'd had a couple of close calls— one at a golf course and one at Afcom. But my luck would change, and my worst nightmare was about to come true.

Chapter 64

Cleared of the underbrush but obsessed with the forest,
Set free from the forest, right back to the forest he runs.
Come, see the person set free who runs right back to
same old chains!
~Dhammapada 344

I got up early, grabbed my bottle of lotion (couldn't leave home without it), then rode my bike all away to UCF, over twelve miles away.

Once I got there, I decided the best place to hide my bike would be in the woods—not with me, but deeper into the woods. That way, after I flashed, I could take off running into the woods and grab it without anyone seeing me. It was the best getaway I could think of.

I went behind the bushes. Man, I was excited. I didn't want to be anywhere else in the world but right there. *Hell yeah. Are you ready, girls?*

The first thing I did was take all my clothes off, except my shoes and socks. I put my T-shirt on my head, folded my pants up nice and neat, then started jacking off with my lotion.

I didn't want to flash the first girl that came by because I wanted to stay there all day.

So, I would wait until right before I decided to leave before flashing. Plus, it had taken me so long to get there, I didn't want to leave so soon.

It was just as fun jacking off while watching them all walk by. I knew I could get anyone of them at any time, but I wasn't in a hurry. I would have loved to flash them all, but I could only flash once because I had to get outta there quick in case they called the cops or told some guys. I damn sure wasn't gonna stick around to find out.

I could sometimes get girls back-to-back if they were close enough to each other, but I wasn't gonna wait more than a minute after the first one because I needed to get gone in a hurry.

I was there for a few hours and could see all the cars that went by. I was always on the lookout, especially for the ones that had sirens on them. Those were the enemy. If I saw one of them coming, I would take off running into the woods until they passed by. I didn't see any that morning, but I did see one car that kinda caught my attention. It was a Ford Crown Victoria with dark-tinted windows that looked like an undercover cop car, but it kept driving by at a regular speed without slowing down or anything, so I just let the thought pass. If it was a cop looking for me, all they would've had to do was pull right up to me, and I would've been caught red-handed.

I forgot about that car and continued doing what I was doing. I decided the next girl who walked by was gonna be the one.

"FREEZE. DON'T MOVE!" Oh my God. There were cops in the woods coming up behind me. They had snuck up on me. I couldn't believe it. *Oh my fucking God.* I had to run. I needed to run. But they were in my fucking way. I couldn't even grab my pants.

I had no choice but to run out into the street toward the campus. They flushed me out of the woods. I couldn't fucking believe it; it was all bad. Even if I got away, I would be without my pants and underwear. Now I was really running for my life.

When I ran across the main street that went to the campus, cars were beeping while the cops were chasing and screaming at me to stop. *Hell no.* I wasn't gonna stop. Were they crazy?

There was no way I could get caught. What would happen if my family found out?

Oh please, God. Let me please get away. I'll never do it again, I promise. Please don't let them catch me.

How would I explain it to my mom?

I crossed the street into another wooded area, then ran down into a ditch and up the other side. I was getting away, but I had to keep running. I couldn't stop.

I came out of those woods and into a student parking lot. I was running by guys and girls who were walking to and from their classes, and I could hear them yelling things at me.

My heart was beating so fucking fast and hard. I needed to find a place to rest, but I couldn't stop.

I lost the cops, but I couldn't believe I was fucking naked. What was I gonna do?

I stopped and hid in between two cars and tried to catch my breath while trying to decide where to run next. I was trapped. I couldn't run anywhere. I needed to get back to those woods to get my pants and bike, but I knew my pants would be gone. I'm sure the cops had grabbed them.

I poked my head up over the top of a car to see if the coast was clear, and I saw that same Crown Victoria. Fuck, they were cops that drove by me but acted like they didn't see me when they drove by. They fucking tricked me.

The Crown Vic was stopped, and cops were talking to some students who pointed in the direction where I was hiding. *Oh God.* I just couldn't run anymore, so I ducked down and tried to hide, but the cops were headed right toward me. That's when I decided right then and there: fuck it. If they saw me, I would just give up. What the hell would I do if I did get away? How would I get all the way back to Winter Springs completely naked? I had even lost my T-shirt when they were chasing me. So when they spotted me, I just put my hands in the air and was surprised that they didn't tackle me. They just opened the back door of their car and told me to get in.

I was taken to the campus police station and given a blanket to cover up.

I knew my life was over.

"Please don't tell my mom," I begged them. "Please let me go. I will never do it again. Please don't tell anyone. They won't put my name in the newspaper, will they?"

The cop said he had no choice; he had to arrest me. He said he couldn't promise me anything, but he said he couldn't lie to me either. He said not only would I be in the newspaper, I would probably be all over the news too.

I couldn't fucking believe what was happening. I was through. My life was over. People were really gonna think I was a weirdo.

After five long years, my secret would finally be revealed.

Chapter 65

It's not good, the doing of the deed
That once it's done, you regret,
whose result you reap crying,
Your face in tears
Dhammapada 67

I was taken to the 33ʳᵈ Street jail in Orlando and charged with indecent exposure. How embarrassing. What was I gonna do? What was my family gonna think of me?

I was too embarrassed to even call my mom for help. Maybe I could get out on bond without anyone knowing, then just go home and pretend nothing ever happened.

My bond was only $500, which meant that I would only have to pay 10 percent of that to get out. Fifty bucks wasn't shit, but I didn't have fifty dollars on me.

Fuck, who could I fucking call? That's when I thought of Robert. He was the only person I knew of who I could call.

I had a brand-new electric guitar that I knew he liked. I could offer him that, so I called him up and told him what happened—pretty much begging and pleading for him to come get me out. I told him I would give him my guitar. I also told him not to say anything to anyone. He really surprised me and said that he would do it when he had a chance, so I gave him a bail bondsman number that was on the wall next to the phone. Then all I could really do after that was just wait and hope that he came through.

The guitar was worth a lot more than $50, so maybe he would do it. I hoped so because getting out on my own recognizance was definitely out of the question.

With my escape from the halfway house and a violation of probation on my record, they obviously didn't trust me to appear in court voluntarily, so bonding out was my only hope.

Come on, Robert. Don't let me down.

God, I hated going through the grueling booking processes of jails. The cells were always freezing, and on top of that, everyone was loud as fuck—bitching, complaining, and crying about getting arrested. So, sleeping was definitely out of the question.

The UCF Campus Police found my clothes and gave them back to me, but I was still freezing my ass off.

God, how did this fucking happen? I couldn't believe I got caught. What was I gonna do? How was I gonna explain it to my mom?

If they put me in the newspaper or on the news, I was getting the hell out of Winter Springs.

I definitely would never be able to flash anywhere near Seminole or Orange County ever again.

They knew who I was now. All they would have to do is come knocking on my door. Yeah, I was gone." *Come on, Robert. Please get me the fuck out of here.*

One of the deputies opened up the refrigerator door and called my name. *Hell, yeah. Please be my bond.* And it was. Robert had actually come through.

I had lost all track of time, but I knew it had to be really late or very early in the morning.

Robert was outside waiting for me when I got released, and I told him to drive me straight home so I could give him the guitar.

Robert thought it was funny that I got caught for something like that, but I didn't think it was funny at all. I was terrified.

All I wanted to do was go straight to my room, lock the door, crawl under my covers, go to sleep, and never wake up. It was all a really bad dream.

As soon as I got home and gave Robert the guitar, that's exactly what I did. I went straight to my room and went to bed.

Thank God my mom and everyone else was asleep because I didn't want to deal with anyone right then. As a matter of fact, I didn't want to deal with anyone ever again.

I just wanted to be left alone forever.

I woke up to the sound of my mom knocking on my bedroom door.

"Go away. I don't want to talk to anyone."

"Come out here, son. I love you. I want to talk to you."

"No."

I stayed in my room until 1 p.m. before finally coming out—only because I was hungry.

My mom already knew what had happened. I don't know how she found out. I guess the cops called and told her. Then I saw she had a newspaper on the kitchen table. Sure enough, I was in it. What could I say?

Not only that, but the phone was ringing off the hook, and the calls weren't from anyone I knew either. They were from girls and gay guys who had read my name in the paper.

I didn't want to talk to them, but my mom would hand me the phone. They were all weirdos wanting me to come over to their house and show my dick to them. They said they wanted to see it, too, and what was I doing later that night.

I took the phone off the hook, then went and sat on the living room couch and cried, especially when my mom sat down next to me, hugged me, and asked why I was doing that at the college. That's when I really broke down and cried even harder.

I told her about the guy in the woods when I was seven, and that's why I was doing the same thing to girls that he did to me. I knew that was why I was doing it. It had to be.

The next words that came out of my mom's mouth, I will never forget.

"Don't let that man destroy your life," she said.

I will never forget her telling me that. It was so true, but it was also much easier said than done because that man would go on to destroy my life for the next thirtysomething years.

I always wondered where I would be or what I would've become had I never encountered that man in the woods.

***

I was out on bond for indecent exposure and on probation for escaping from the halfway house and who knows what else. I was surprised they even let me out on bond, so I knew when I went to court that they were gonna lock me up again. That's when I made up my mind. There was no way in hell I was going back to court. I also felt ashamed, humiliated, and embarrassed to even live at home.

My covers had been pulled. I couldn't live in Winter Springs any longer. There was no fucking way.

I would just hitchhike back to California. I didn't care about not having any money. I knew how to hustle now. There were plenty of gay guys that would pick me up, so that's what I decided to do. Plus, it would be fun to see if I could hitchhike all the way to California—with no money and just the clothes on my back.

I called Robert, told him my plan, and asked if he could give me a ride to the rest area in Longwood, on I-4, just east of Highway 434. A lot of trucks stopped there, so I knew I could get a ride to Jacksonville. Then I could take Interstate 10 all the way to Los Angeles.

Robert thought I was fucking crazy. I told him I'd done it before, and it wasn't that hard.

It was also the only choice I had. I wasn't sticking around there any longer. Why? So I could go to court and go back to jail? Fuck that. I'm gone.

***

Robert dropped me off at the rest area, and the first thing I noticed was the smell of semi-trucks. Ahh, the smell of diesel. I loved that fucking smell. It was the smell of freedom for me. Yes, take me away. Get me as far away from Winter Springs and Orlando as possible.

I went to use the restroom, then to the vending machines to get a soda and some chips, then headed to the on-ramp to wait for a ride. Damn, I didn't even get to finish my Coke and chips before a car stopped to pick me up. *Wow! That was quick.*

I decided that everyone who gave me a ride I was gonna ask for money.

I was just gonna say that I didn't have any money, and whatever they could spare would be greatly appreciated because I was really hungry. Plus, I needed to build some money up.

The first car that picked me up was going to Daytona, which was where I needed to go anyway to get on I-95 north, so I could take that to Jacksonville.

The guy that picked me up was normal. I'll refer to people as normal if they didn't do anything weird or strange, so he was normal. I told him what I was doing, and he also thought I was nuts. I didn't have a backpack, duffel bag, or even a toothbrush. All I had was 80 cents in my pocket. I was the one who wasn't normal, and I was judging people who picked me up, deciding whether they were weird or not. Ha-ha. I'm the weird one.

I asked the guy if he could help me out with a couple bucks, and he gave me a five-dollar bill.

Then he dropped me off on Main Street, right on the beach in Daytona. That's when I decided, what the hell, I might as well spend a day at the beach before heading to Jacksonville. I was in no hurry, plus I had $5.80 on me. I could get something to eat at McDonald's. I decided to walk over to the boardwalk to find somewhere to sit so I could watch all the pretty girls walk by.

I felt so free. I didn't have a worry in the world. No more probation, no court, and no job to worry about. I just wanted to go somewhere far away, whcrc nobody kncw who I was.

I loved the smell of the salty ocean air, which gave me the idea to walk out to the ocean and put my feet in it. Then, when I got to California, I would do the same thing— just to say I made it from coast to coast, from the Atlantic all away to the Pacific.

Chapter 66

Here I go again on my own
Going down that only road I've ever known
Like a drifter I was born to walk alone
~ White Snake

The reason I chose to run away to California is pretty simple—several reasons, really.

As a teenager in Florida in the '80s, everyone wanted to run away to California and become a movie star. But, in my case, I wanted to be a porn star.

I also remember seeing David Lee Roth's music video, "California Girls," and wanted to go see all the beautiful woman on the beaches that I always saw on TV.

I also wanted to get as far away from Florida as possible after my arrest.

I was so ashamed and embarrassed. I felt like a pariah, so I knew California would be the

perfect place for me, especially after I learned how to hustle gay men. I knew that I

would not have a problem surviving out there.

Once I arrived in California and discovered San Luis Obispo and saw all the beautiful CalPoly girls, then found out they had a nude beach—yep, that's when I knew that

I had found my home. College girls, nude beaches, and gay men. Sign me up.

Chapter 67

It took me only two rides to get to the Pirate's Cove parking lot. Wow! I was amazed at the view. What a beautiful place. I should have brought all my stuff with me. I could have camped out there. I walked over to a man who I saw sitting in his car and asked him where the nude beach was. He pointed and said I had to hike down to it.

I was too scared to go, but I could see people down there, and sure enough, they were naked, but they were too far away from where I was standing, so I was cool with just staying in the parking lot for the time being. Imagine me, too scared to go on to a nude beach. I didn't understand myself sometimes. Explain that. I didn't know it at the time, but I would end up becoming a regular down there, and it would end up being my favorite beach of all time. A lot of crazy shit was also gonna happen to me down there that I'll get to in a bit, but what would be even crazier was that Pirate's Cove and I would make nationwide headlines twenty-one years from that moment, so stay tuned.

***

I sat on a big rock in the Pirate's Cove parking lot, enjoying the amazing view. I also did some roaming around and found a giant cave at the end of the trail that led toward the beach, which was big enough to drive a car into and overlooked the ocean, which was really cool.

I could tell people made campfires there by the look of the charred walls. It would be a perfect place for me to camp out, but the only problem was there weren't any stores anywhere near there. I went back out to the parking lot to see who I could meet. I noticed a lot of guys sitting in their cars. Maybe I found the perfect place after all. I sat back down on that rock and hoped that one of the older guys sitting in their car was gay and would pounce on me pretty quick because I needed some damn money. I also noticed a lot of guys coming in and out of the bushes next to the parking lot and wondered where they were going. That's when an old man in his sixties got out of his car and started walking toward me with his hands in his pockets, pretending to be enjoying the view. To make a long story short, I made forty bucks that day and also gained a lot of valuable information. The old man told me that the beach was a cruising spot for gays. He also said that all the guys going in and out of the bushes were gay and were going in there to either suck dick or get fucked. He said there was a smaller separate beach where all the gays went, but you had to climb down a rope to get to it. He gave me a good rundown of everything.

Yes, I found the perfect place to hang out for a while. I decided I would hitchhike back and forth from San Luis Obispo to Pirate's every day and sleep in those woods by the creek. I would just do that until I met an older guy that met all my criteria—who I felt comfortable with and who would give me a place to stay, at least long enough so I could accumulate some money and then steal his car. *Hell yeah.* I was getting excited. I knew it would just be a matter of time before I had a pocketful of money and a car. I had a lot of places I wanted to flash. That was my number-one priority. I didn't give a fuck about anything else. I wanted to flash all the girls I could. I wanted to check out every college campus, every beach strand, every woman's clothing store, every apartment complex swimming pool, weight room, laundry room, shoe store, yogurt and ice cream shop. My list of places was getting bigger by the day. And not having a car was killing me. My urges were really strong. I felt like I was being tied down without a car.

Meeting Vicky helped control my urges temporarily. Guys sucking my dick also helped. But the first chance I had to steal a car, I was gone. Having sex with pretty girls and getting my dick sucked by guys just wasn't the same as flashing unsuspecting women. Flashing was way more exciting and adrenaline-pumping. I just can't explain it. It's one hell of an addiction, and I couldn't see myself ever wanting to stop. It was an amazing rush—ten times better than cocaine, alcohol, acid, or any other drug I had ever tried. What the hell had happened to me? What had my life become? I knew from an early age that something was wrong with me. Who does this? Nobody I'd ever known. I knew it wasn't normal. But why did it have to happen to me, being cursed with an addiction that I fucking enjoyed so much? It was fucking crazy; it was almost like I was born to do it.

Why did I have to have a big dick? I'm not huge, but I'm definitely not small. I always wondered how I would've become a flasher if I had a little dick. It just wouldn't have worked. As a matter of fact, if I had a little dick, I wouldn't be in prison right now writing this book because I would've never got the cops called on me. All the women would have just laughed and said, "Aaaahhh, how cute," and just kept walking. You have to have a big dick to be a flasher. How else are you gonna get that ultimate shock value? So instead of having girls laugh and just walk away, I have them running and screaming, telling me how sick, disgusting and perverted I am on their way to the nearest phone to call the police.

Chapter 68

Of all the experiences I've had sleeping with gay guys in their beds, they were all the same. Here's what I couldn't stand. For one, they didn't sleep. They just lay there and waited for me to move. Because as soon as I would move and try to get more comfortable, they would take that as a cue that I must be awake, and their hands would make a beeline for my dick. I hated that shit when I was trying to sleep. And there was no way in hell I could sleep on my back because my dick would be easier for them to get to, so I would always lay in bed completely frozen and afraid to fucking move. Because if I moved, they would think, "Oh, he must be awake now. Let's try to suck his dick."

Leave me the fuck alone. Let me fucking sleep. I hated that shit. They would never let me sleep. That's when I learned that I had to sleep on my stomach. But they would still try to wedge their hand under there and grab my dick every time I moved. I couldn't stand to be woken up when I was trying to sleep. That would piss me off so much. And, God forbid, I wake up with a hard-on because I had to pee. That's when they go into full attack mode. "Oh, he must be really horny because his dick is so hard." They automatically assumed I needed to be taken care of.

They would say, "Come here. Let me take care of that big thing."

No, I don't need to be taken care of. I need to piss, asshole, and thanks for keeping me up all night, reaching for my dick every time I fucking moved.

I would rather sleep in the bushes and not get bothered so fucking much.

Chapter 69

I really blended in with college kids because I was the same age. All I was missing was a backpack slung over my shoulder. Nobody even looked at me twice. I looked just like them, except I was in my own little world and on an entirely different planet.

I got to the apartments and saw a blonde with a backpack and decided to follow her from a safe distance. She cut through the apartment parking lot, walked toward the back, and turned off into the woods on a little trail. *What the hell?* My heart was really racing as I followed her. The trail led to a completely isolated wooded area. I couldn't believe it. It led to a creek that you had to cross to continue on the trail. There were rocks that were strategically placed in the water that was maybe a foot deep that the students used to cross over to the other side.

The hot little blonde was all by herself in the woods, and my urges were out of control. All kinds of shit ran through my mind. What a perfect spot to just whip my dick out and start jacking off while girls were trying to cross the creek. I noticed when she was crossing the creek, she would be looking down, watching her steps, so all I had to do was be waiting on the other side with my pants down with a hard-on. What a perfect fucking spot. And talk about secluded.

I didn't have to worry about any bystanders seeing me. My adrenaline was through the roof. I walked back toward the apartments just to watch the entrance to the trail from a distance. It was fucking perfect. It seemed like a girl walked through there every ten minutes. There were a few guys I had to be careful of, but most of the girls were alone. And every one of them uses the trail. *Wow!*

I decided to follow the rest of that trail to see where it came out at. After crossing the creek, it went through a little bit more wooded area and then came out onto another apartment complex parking lot, which then led to the campus right by the Cal Poly stadium.

Man, I was in fucking heaven. I couldn't believe my luck at finding that spot.

I was just missing two things: a getaway car and some lotion—the two most important tools of my trade. I put that spot on the top of my list and kept walking, which was really hard.

I wanted to go back there so bad and flash one of those sexy-ass girls. It was so hard to control myself. I walked by the stadium, and I was actually on campus, so I started roaming all over the place. Not too many good flashing spots on campus. Way too much foot traffic. People all over the damn place. I liked seclusion. I still couldn't get over that creek. It was a flasher's dream. College girls all alone in the woods. Yeah, I was going to get them all, one at a time. It had the perfect getaway too. All I had to do was flash them, run out of the woods, through the apartment complex, then to my car, which they would never see me get into. I would be long gone before they even got close to a phone or were able to tell anyone. I couldn't fucking wait.

***

I knew I was taking too big of a risk by flashing so many girls there. I'm sure one of the girls had to have called the police. Right as all that was going through my mind, I about had a heart attack when I looked out onto the street and saw a cop car. *Oh shit.* And I was completely naked with a T-shirt on my head, a bottle of lotion in one hand, and a hard dick in the other.

I started praying, *Please keep driving by. Don't stop. Please keep going. God, I hope he didn't see me.*

As I was watching, he got about 100 yards down the road and hit his brake lights.

Oh my God, This can't be happening. There was no reason for him to hit his brake lights right there. Then my biggest fear came true. He did a U-turn and started heading back toward me.

There was no doubt in my mind he was coming after me.

I was terrified, so I grabbed all my clothes and took off running across the field toward the apartments. I had to jump a big chain link fence to get into the apartments, but first, I had to put my clothes back on.

Nobody in the world can get dressed while running as fast as they can. Especially when I looked back toward the bushes and saw the cop watching me from there. He didn't even try to chase me because I was too far away from him. But I knew one thing for sure. He was on his radio.

As soon as I jumped the fence and started to run to where my truck was parked, I saw another cop car coming through the parking lot of the apartments, and he saw me. *Motherfucker.* I couldn't even get to my truck. I was fucked, so I ran through the apartments, not knowing where to go. All I could think about was that I needed to get to the other side of Santa Rosa Street so I could run and hide at the old man's house.

I knew it was just a matter of time before the cops would be swarming all over the place like a bunch of bees. I needed to get the fuck out of there. As I was trying to run across Santa Rosa Street, I was cussing at all the cars." Get the fuck out of my way, I need to get across the fucking street."

Remember that game Frogger by Atari? Picture that game on the highest, fastest level. That was me trying to get across Santa Rosa Street.

I had made it to the little cement center median without getting run over. People were beeping at me, and I was cussing at them. I wasn't worried about them. I was worried about cop cars seeing me before I crossed. But it took me ten seconds too long. Because I looked to my right and saw a cop coming from the north at a high rate of speed, with its lights flashing while I was still standing on the median.

I found just enough gap in traffic for my skinny ass to fit through and took off. But it was too late. The cop saw me. I tried running, but I knew I was through. I was out of breath and couldn't run anymore. I wasn't going to get away, especially after I tripped and fell. So I just lay there, cussing myself for going back there so many times. What a fucking stupid idiot. I was in big trouble. I knew I was going to be all over the news. I'm sure they had been looking for me for a while.

I flashed so many girls in San Luis Obispo that I lost count. All I could do was pray that most of them didn't call the police. Even if half of them called, I would still end up being in jail for a long time. Yep, I was done. Game over.

Chapter 70

I've had more trouble with myself
than with any man I've ever met.
~ Dwight Moody

They took me to the San Luis Obispo Police Department, where all the cops were acting like they had captured the most famous person in America. They put me in an ice-cold holding cell that was only meant to hold one person—with no mattress or blankets. All I had on were my shorts and T-shirt, and I was freezing my butt off.

The door had a little square window in it, so the cops could look in at me. I was in that cell for at least three hours, and every single cop who worked at that police station, and who knows who else, had to come look in that window at me. They all had to see what a flasher looked like. Twelve different people looked in that window.

I felt like an exhibit at a zoo. "Come on, everybody. You have to look at this rare flasher. He must have migrated here from the East Coast because they were rarely found in California, especially on the central coast. We're assuming he must be from the central part of Florida. Or somewhere in that region. There are very few of them left in the world."

That's what I felt like sitting in there. A fucking exhibit.

Then the depression kicked in. I thought about my family. Why couldn't I be normal like everyone else? How long was it gonna go on? Would I ever be happy and live a normal life?

Or would I always just be considered a weirdo and be locked up in cages my whole life like an animal in a zoo?

That's when I just put my head in my hands and cried. I prayed. *Lord, why me? Why me? Why me?*

Next thing I knew, my cell door was opening, and a detective wanted me to come out so he could take some pictures, which was part of the booking process.

Then he made the strangest request. He wanted me to put my T-shirt on my head.

I immediately refused. "No, I'm not doing it. No." All the cops thought that was funny. But I refused to be humiliated any more than I already was. Fuck them. They got who they were looking for. They didn't need any more proof than what they already had. Let them figure the rest out by themselves.

My biggest fear when I would go to jail was other inmates finding out my charges.

So, I would always lie and tell them I was in there for something else.

I found out the inmates hated sex offenders—even though sex offenders came in different forms. I didn't like being labeled a child molester or rapist because I wasn't either of those. I was just a flasher. But the shallow-minded inmates in the jails didn't see it that way. They just assumed all sex offenders were child molesters.

So, I was really terrified of going to court and somebody from my cell going with me. Those were always stressful times.

But when I was all over the news and in the newspapers, it was hard to lie about my charges. So, I was kinda screwed. But I was lucky that time because nobody in the jail found out about my charges.

But the bad news was that Florida had a warrant for me for escape and violation of probation.

I was not looking forward to being extradited all way back there, chained up, and shackled in a van with about ten other inmates. That was not fun at all. It was actually a nightmare because they had to stop at every fucking county jail in America.

***

I always wondered where I would be and what I would be doing if that incident had never happened to me when I was seven years old.

Would I have finished school?

Would I have gone to college?

What career path would I have chosen?

Where would I be living? Would I be happy?

Why was I cursed with such a fucked up addiction?

I asked myself those questions all the time. But I never know the answers.

I have always believed that everything in life happens for a reason.

The reason for my life, I have yet to figure out. But I will let you know as soon as I know where all this chaos is going to lead me.

***

I hated stealing, but I just couldn't help it.

The only reason I stole from people was so I could flash.

But it really bothered me, especially when people tried to help me.

Flashing was all I cared about, and it was all I wanted to do.

Every car that I would end up stealing in my life would be for that reason, and that reason only, so I could flash.

It was also the reason I stole money, jewelry, and other valuables—so I would be able to pay for the gas to put in the cars, so I could drive around and flash.

My addiction caused me to be a thief, just like a drug addict steals to support their habit.

I know I would've never become a thief if it wasn't for my addiction.

I hated stealing, and I hate people who do.

So, I guess you could say I hate myself, which I do. I hate myself when I'm flashing, I hate myself for stealing, I hate myself for hurting people, I hate myself for going to jail, I hate myself for not being able to live a normal life, I hate myself for all kinds of things.

In my heart, I want to be a good person, do the right things, and never hurt anyone, but my goddamn, fucked up mind won't let me.

My addiction is kicking my ass. It's killing me, and I just can't control it.

Chapter 71

I ended up at the Seminole County Jail in Sanford, Florida, for all the warrants I had out for my arrest.

It was crazy because even going to jail didn't stop my addiction. I would flash jail guards, nurses, counselors, or any other female staff that worked there. And what made it really nice was that most of the time, I wouldn't even get in trouble for it.

What were they gonna do? Throw me in jail?

Plus, there were a lot of sexy-ass deputies that worked in the jails. I would get them all.

Chapter 72

The first time I ever tried to get help for my addiction was in the Orange County jail in Santa Ana, California. I put in a request to see the psychologist. I was really disgusted with my life and really wanted help. I just wanted to live a normal life, so I wanted to talk to someone to see if anything could be done. I was in jail for flashing at a Clothestime store, among other places all over Orange County.

I was called into the head psychiatrist's office and regretted it right away. I was told to have a seat in the chair in front of his desk. The doctor was an older guy in his late fifties or early sixties. I knew right away he was gay. He didn't act all flamboyant, but I knew that he was. My gaydar was pretty damn good. Then my suspicions were confirmed when he gave me a magazine and told me to read a certain article. The article was about gay men and their lifestyles. It was fucking weird. Why was he having me read that? I felt really uncomfortable. The article was really sexual in nature. He was probably jacking off behind his desk while I was reading it. What did it have to do with me trying to get help for flashing? He made me feel really uncomfortable, so I told him I was good. I just wanted to go back to my cell and talk to someone else. It was really strange. It was like he got excited about my charges. He even made a joke about it. Who the fuck was he? He was the head psychiatrist in the jail? What a fucking joke. Nothing about my crimes was funny, and I didn't go into his office to hear his smart-ass comments or to turn him on by reading his gay fucking article. I got the fuck out of there and told him I would talk to another psychologist.

The following week I had much better luck. Not only was the psychologist super fine, but she was understanding, caring, and really good. I wish I could remember her name because she understood what I was going through and really wanted to help me. She was a blonde in her twenties and really fucking pretty. She ended up calling me into her office once a week. I really thought about flashing her, but I just couldn't because she was genuinely concerned about me and really wanted to help. I just couldn't do that to her. So, I just jacked off in the shower thinking about her every day. She had me on a 12-step program that I worked on in her office every week. But instead of alcohol being the addiction, she told me to change the alcohol into the urge to flash or something like that. She would also talk to me for an hour once a week. She was definitely in her job to help people, that's for sure. I have dealt with plenty of psychologists who I could tell didn't give a fuck. They were just at jails and prisons to collect a check. I wish I knew where she was now because she was really good. But it seemed like the only time I really wanted to get help was when I was locked up. Because when I was out flashing, getting help was the last thing on my mind.

Chapter 73

Not only did I have a son that I couldn't be a father to. I also met a beautiful Puerto Rican woman I dated for a few months and had a daughter by—who I would also never be a father to. All because of my addiction. I just couldn't stay in a relationship. My heart has always been in the right place, and I wanted to live a normal life and be in a normal relationship, but my addiction would always rear its ugly head, and I would have to get away and flash.

Their mothers never knew I had this addiction. They just thought I had left them, which made me a horrible person and father who didn't care about his kids.

To them, I was just a deadbeat dad who would spend his life in and out of jails and prisons. There was no telling what else they told my kids as they were growing up without me in their lives.

That really tore me up my entire life because I wasn't that person.

I'd always told myself that if I ever had kids, I would never leave them like my real father left me when I was two. But there I was, history repeating itself.

Now my kids were going to grow up not knowing who their dad was.

I cursed my addiction constantly.

I would always look up at the sky with tears in my eyes, wondering if there was a god. Why wasn't he helping me? Why was he doing this to me? What did I do to deserve this?

Fuck it. Oh well, there's nothing I could really do. It is what it is.

I would just have to believe what I've always believed in, that everything happens for a reason.

I couldn't wait to see why God was putting me through all of this pain and torture. What was His reason? I couldn't wait to find out. Or would I just be saying that my entire life until I died without anything at all happening? I didn't even think I believed in God. I didn't know what the fuck to believe in.

It seemed like every time I went to prison, my sentences became longer. This next incident would give me an even bigger prison sentence.

***

I was in San Diego, all high on crystal meth. This was around the time I discovered Viagra, which was a wonderful flashing drug. Even better than meth, so I had popped one of those.

I was on a really good spree. I was just driving around looking for new places and discovered Scripps Ranch High School by accident.

The student lot was across the street from the school in a dirt lot, which was the perfect setup, away from the school, all by itself. It also had the perfect getaway for me. There was a dried-up creek bed next to the lot, and on the other side of that was an industrial complex where I could hide my van.

I was so fucking excited. It was the best and most secluded high school parking lot I'd ever been to. I was definitely going to flash a high school girl before I left there for sure.

My dick was rock fucking hard as I was putting lotion on it, walking across the creek toward the parking lot.

I was so excited; they were the moments I lived for. I loved perfect spots with perfect getaways, especially when hot high school girls were involved. And I was getting ready to flash the hottest one ever.

I couldn't believe my luck when I saw her walking across the street, coming toward the parking lot. I couldn't have asked for a better opportunity. She was leaving school early for some reason.

Oh my fucking God. I could tell she was fine from a mile away. Dammit, she was fucking tall, close to six feet, with blond hair and wearing really tight Dickies pants that were low on her waist. I could see her stomach and pierced belly button. Got damn, she was sexy as fuck.

Girls didn't look or dress like that when I was in high school.

She also looked well over eighteen. I thought she was just dropping something off for someone.

But I didn't know or care.

I couldn't fucking believe it was just her and me all alone in the lot.

She didn't see me because I was hiding behind other cars.

She was walking toward the middle of the lot. Thank God for the meth and Viagra, or I would've cum all over my-self. Because the closer she got, the finer she was. She was fucking perfect.

She had nice tits, perfect ass, a flat stomach, pierced belly button, blonde hair, and looked taller than me. She was definitely going to be a memorable one if I could control myself long enough.

I took all my clothes off and threw them on the ground right before I saw her get into a blue Honda Accord.

I walked over to the front of her car as fast as I could, just as she was getting in it.

I loved these fucking moments, with the sun beating down on me as I was waving it at her.

Then she did the one thing she shouldn't have. She sat there and watched. She didn't lay on the horn or even try to drive away. It was just her and me in the parking lot, and she gave me plenty of time, so I walked over to her driver's window that was rolled up, and gave her a closeup. And she still just stared at me. Then she locked her doors and continued to watch.

God, she was a perfect fucking ten. She was fucking hot.

That was when I felt the inevitable. Oh fuck, I was starting to cum. So I started to jack off.

"Yeah, watch this, baby." I think I came more than I ever have in my life all over her fucking window while imagining it was her face that was just inches away. Then I walked back to the front of her car, still hard as a rock, and waved it at her one last time before I ran like hell to my clothes.

It was definitely one of my all-time favorites. But it would also end up being one of my all-time biggest mistakes and nightmares.

Because several months later, I would be arrested in Oklahoma and be told that I had a warrant in San Diego County for rape.

"WHAT?" I knew it had to be a mistake. I would never touch a girl, let alone rape one, so I knew they had the wrong person. I wasn't really worried, as I was being extradited back to San Diego. Then they told me what it was all about that I assaulted a girl in the Scripps Ranch parking lot.

That's when I started to get really scared, but I knew I had never touched her. I would find out later that the cops told her to say that I touched her, so it would sound more serious, and they would be able to pursue me and catch me faster, whatever that meant.

They found out who I was through DNA from her window.

I ended up taking that case all the way to trial because I was facing fifteen years in prison for something I knew I didn't do.

It was just amazing how corrupt cops could be to make her lie like that.

But I had a public defender who was the best lawyer I've ever had. He got her on the stand and made her admit that I had never touched her, which was the truth. I knew I deserved to go to jail for flashing her, but I didn't deserve to go to prison for fifteen years for something I didn't do.

It was the scariest moment of my life going through that trial.

I did get prison time because she was seventeen at the time, I think she was like two weeks away from turning eighteen when I flashed her. I also got charged for all the other indecent exposures I did in San Diego County. My misery was just never going to cnd.

Chapter 74

I had a lot of time to reflect while I was in jail. I thought about my son and daughter a lot. I wanted so badly to be a part of their lives, and it just killed me that I couldn't.

I hated everything about my addiction. I was just disgusted with myself. I wanted to change so badly for my kids. I wanted to have my own place so they could visit me. I wanted a normal job. I hated always being on the run with warrants out for my arrest. I didn't want to spend my whole life hustling gays, and I definitely didn't want to spend my whole life flashing.

I just hated hurting so many people, especially people that loved me. I wanted to do something with my life. I was so tired of living the way I was living. It fucking sucked. I was either going to kill myself or spend the rest of my life in jail and prison.

My addiction was killing me. It was just so hard for me to stop. I stopped using crystal meth without any problem. I quit drinking without any problem. But I just couldn't stop flashing.

Chapter 75

I had just gotten out of prison and was homeless, living in San Luis Obispo. I was trying to get my life together. I had gotten a job at the BMW dealership, bought a van that was actually registered to me and was working on getting my own apartment. It was the best I'd ever done. The only thing that sucked was that I had to wear an ankle monitor, which I did not like. But I knew parole would never go away, so I was trying to deal with it the best I could.

Then, after about three months, my addiction reared its ugly head. I was almost forty-five years old and still couldn't stop. I still couldn't get over the power of my addiction. But I was about to experience something I had never experienced before. I always believed everything happens for a reason. I never knew what the reason was most of the time. But I was in for a really big shock that I would've never discovered if I didn't do what I did in front of the Pismo outlets while sitting in my van.

It was crazy. It would be a curse but also a blessing in disguise. Maybe there was a God making me do all the things I was doing. I think he was leading me somewhere, but I didn't like the way he was going about it. He was definitely testing my patience. I didn't know how much more I could handle. He was really testing and pushing me to see how much I could take. I had already been on the edge of several cliffs, ready to go off of them. Why was he stopping me? I'd had enough.

I sat in my van and cried while praying. I couldn't believe my addiction was so fucking powerful. I had a pair of scissors in my hand, fighting back tears and pain. I didn't want to do it. But then again, I did. I thought about all the people I was going to hurt and let down. I had promised my son and my family that I wouldn't go back to prison. And I was about to fuck all that up with one cut of the scissors. I was crying, asking God why he was putting me through this. But he wouldn't fucking answer me. I didn't know whether I wanted to slice my wrists or cut my monitor off. I just wanted to end my pain and suffering.

But what bothered me the most was hurting other people, especially the ones who loved me. I just want them to know that I don't enjoy it one bit. I don't love going to jail and prison. But what hurt me the most was when my phone started ringing at that very moment, and I saw who it was. Oh my God. Of all people. It was my son. I was sick to my stomach. I knew it was God's divine intervention, telling me, "Don't do it. You're going to lose this little guy right here. He needs you."

I was too distraught to answer it. It would've killed me to hear his voice. I took the battery out of my phone and threw it onto the passenger's side floorboard while cursing my addiction once again. After about a half hour of having the scissors in my hand, I reached down and cut my monitor off. And at that moment, I knew my life was over.

I jumped out of the van and ran to the bus stop that I was parked next to, threw my monitor into a garbage can, then jumped back in my van and got the fuck out of there.

I got on the 101 south and headed for Santa Barbara. My misery was never going to end.

Here I fucking go again. I did not like the feeling I was having. All the other times I had cut my monitor off, I had a sense of freedom and excitement, but this time that was all gone.

I was absolutely disgusted with myself. I was going through severe depression.

I rolled down my window and threw my phone out, followed by the battery.

I looked at my van that I was so happy to get and knew it no longer belonged to me. Nothing in it belonged to me because as soon as I got pulled over. It would all be gone.

I couldn't believe I had let so many people down once again.

But the weirdest thing that I felt was that my urges and desires were not there like they were supposed to be. Don't get me wrong, I was still going to flash, but that adrenaline-pumping excitement I was supposed to have was gone.

I felt more suicidal than I've ever felt in my life.

I had $1,700 to my name. And I made the decision that as soon as that money was gone, I would kill myself. I wasn't fucking around this time. And I knew exactly how I was going to do it. I was going to go down to Del Mar, where the Amtrak train ran right along the beach by the cliffs, and I was going to stand on the tracks and let the train end my misery.

I even broke a promise to my own son. What kind of man would do that? I made myself sick.

I was too ashamed to even call or talk to my family ever again. Or anyone else, for that matter.

It was definitely going to be my last spree, and I fucking meant it.

If you don't believe it, fucking watch me. I'm going out with a fucking bang.

But in the meantime, I was going to flash every girl I could, even though my desire wasn't there. I had to flash.

I thought about turning around and going back to San Luis Obispo and telling my parole officer I had made a mistake, but I couldn't do that. I even thought about driving to North Carolina and turning myself in there so my family could hold my van for me. No, I couldn't do that either.

I went too far. I did what I did for a reason.

I had never felt so low in my life. I just didn't care about anything, not even flashing.

I tried to remember my mom's words to stay strong. But I just couldn't see the point. Stay strong for what?

When I got to Santa Barbara, I tried to get into a whole different frame of mind.

I might as well make my last spree a memorable one and go out with a bang before they scrape my ass off the railroad tracks.

I was back to my old perverted self and went on a major flashing spree all over Southern California. But I could feel it. That desire was gone. It wasn't the same. Maybe it was my age. I always wondered if age would cure my addiction. And I think it does.

I felt like I was just going through the motions, just flashing because I was on the run, and I knew I'd go back to prison when I got caught. I was just flashing as many girls as I could.

I was making it my farewell tour.

I was kind of hoping I would get arrested before I ran out of money. Because I really felt that my next prison term would be my last. But how was I going to explain that to the next judge I saw." Really judge, I'm never going to flash again; my desire is gone."

Then I thought to myself, *You're getting old, Pat. It's time to find another hobby.*

But I did have a lot of memorable experiences on that spree.

I couldn't wait to see the headlines when I ran out of money.

"Naked man jacking off on tracks, hit and killed by Amtrak train."

That's the legacy I'm going to leave behind for my kids to remember me by.

They will be so proud of me.

But I know I will be doing everyone a favor. I've never been a father, son, brother, or anything else for that matter. Nobody will miss me or even care.

That's how I was feeling during that last spree. I continued going through extreme depression.

I was so distraught; I didn't even know I had missed my forty-fifth birthday. I didn't even care.

I knew my mom called me on that day, and that made me even more depressed. I knew she was concerned because I hadn't called her in over a week. And I stopped answering my phone. She knew I was in trouble. I would probably never see or hear from her ever again. I just couldn't stay strong any longer. I was getting weaker by the day and running out of strength.

Chapter 76

I obviously don't watch the news while I'm out flashing. But after terrorizing Southern California—from Redondo Beach, to Riverside, Temecula, Brea, Newport Beach, Del Mar, San Diego, back up to Thousand Oaks, and Marina Del Rey—I started to get very paranoid. People started looking at me everywhere I went. And that's when I knew I must be all over the news.

I was constantly aware of my surroundings at all times, and I was very aware of every person who was anywhere near me. And I knew that the way people were looking at me wasn't normal.

It all started when I was standing in front of a Macy's and saw two girls in a car drive by, pointing at me. I walked away, and they tried to follow me.

I had a feeling I was being closed in on. They must've had a very good description of me.

It was happening everywhere I went.

Like I said before, I have great gut instincts. And I knew I was being hunted. I wasn't fucking stupid. Everywhere I went, people were looking at me. I knew my days were numbered.

I was jacking off and flashing so much that my dick was starting to get sore.

I felt it burn every time I put lotion on it, which fucking sucked because I had to stop flashing for a couple of days to let it heal. So, I made it a point to cum one last time before I took a break.

I was in a parking lot of a fitness center and jacked off in front of a girl walking to her car. This would end up being my last flashing incident ever.

She obviously freaked out and told me how fucking disgusting I was as she ran toward the front doors of the fitness center."

Yeah, I know. I'm fucking sick and disgusting, but you're still fine as hell.

And that was it.

Chapter 77

Talk about sick and disgusting. That's exactly how I felt as I got in my van and drove away. I was sick and disgusted with my fucking self. I looked down at my soaked, lotion- and cum-drenched shorts and couldn't wait to kill myself. God, what a fucking weirdo-ass loser I was. I couldn't wait to die and end my misery. What a miserable existence I was living.

I violated my parole and fucked off my life so I could flash. But now I couldn't even do that. I just wanted to cut my dick off and throw it out the damn window and bleed to fucking death. I hated my fucking life. I decided to head to Del Mar right then and there to end my misery, so

I got on the freeway and wasn't even on it for five minutes because I had to get off at an exit to turn around and head back north. That's when all hell broke loose at a red light.

Two cars slammed on their brakes on both sides of me. There was a truck in front of me and another car behind me. And within a matter of seconds, cops jumped out of all those vehicles and had guns pointed at me from every direction—screaming, "POLICE, PUT YOUR FUCKING HANDS UP." All my windows were rolled up and my doors were all locked. They were trying to get in my van but couldn't. All I could think about was my wallet under the seat. I fucking couldn't go to jail without it. Then I thought about making them shoot me. It was the perfect opportunity for me to commit suicide by cop. So, I started to reach under my seat to pretend I had a gun. I would get blasted for sure because my wallet was black and would look like a gun to them. Then I thought about punching the gas and ramming into the truck and the cops in front of me. That would be instant death too.

I was thinking, *Come on, Pat. If you want to end your miserable life so bad, now's the perfect time to do it.* It didn't get any better. It was guaranteed death. I would have six cops all shooting me at once. Fuck yeah, end my fucking misery, it was the perfect time for me to die. So I started reaching for my wallet gun and got my hand on it, when the cop at my driver's window screamed, "DON'T DO IT."

That was the moment I knew I just didn't have it in me. I couldn't commit suicide. For some reason, I didn't want to die. For some crazy-ass reason, I wanted to keep living.

So, I put my hands back up in the air, and they were screaming at me to unlock my doors.

But how was I supposed to do that with my hands in the air? That's when a cop started banging on my window, trying to break it with his gun. I've never been so scared in my life. I really thought I was going to get shot. I then reached for the button on the door to unlock it for them. That's when more hell broke loose. I obviously wasn't resisting, but they damn sure acted like I was. Instead of letting me get out the driver's side, two cops pulled me all the way across and out the passenger side and beat the shit out of me for no reason. Using their favorite words, "Stop resisting, stop resisting," I never once resisted. That's why

I hated them motherfuckers. I should have ran their asses over and made them shoot me.

But I guess I was meant to live.

Chapter 78

Relationships are destroyed because one's addiction
is more important than the people they love.
Success is destroyed because one's addiction
is more important than a job.
Health is destroyed because one's addiction
is more important than their body.
Their whole life is destroyed because addiction
is more important than anything else.

I knew once I got arrested that I would be facing the longest prison term I'd ever had.

I had indecent exposures all over San Diego, Orange, LA, and Ventura Counties. And every one of those counties wanted me. It all came out to ten years and eight months. My sentences just kept getting longer and longer. But this last sentence didn't really bother me as much because I knew it had happened for a reason. I felt in my heart that it was my last time ever going to prison.

From the moment I cut that bracelet off and started flashing in Santa Barbara and felt that the urge and desire were gone, I knew it would be my last flashing spree. So, as I sat in prison, I had a sense of relief and happiness. I also never wanted to experience that depressing feeling ever again. It was the most suicidal I have ever felt in my life.

It was during this prison term that I decided I wanted to write this book about my life. I wanted my kids to know why I was never there for them. I wanted to tell them in my own words because their mothers never knew about my addiction, so there was no telling what they said to them about me. I'm sure they told them that I didn't love them because I was never there. All I can do is tell them the truth and hope that they will forgive me for not being there for them. I can't change my past, but I can sure try to change my present and my future.

When your mind is in the right place, and your intentions are sincere, good things will happen. I was in a whole different mindset while I was in prison. I really wanted to change my life. I just didn't want to keep living the way I was. I was getting older, and I was tired of spending my whole life behind bars. I'd spent over half my life locked up. It just wasn't fun anymore.

I wanted to live a normal life and be there for my kids. And speaking of my kids, the greatest thing happened to me while I was in prison that would really change my life. *Hell yeah, hell yeah, hell fuckin yeah.* It's all I ever wanted.

* * *

My daughter wrote me, my daughter wrote me, my daughter wrote me.

I couldn't fucking believe it. She was around fourteen years old; it was the first time I'd ever heard from her. I cried with joy before I even opened the letter. God, I was so excited, I couldn't believe it.

I made up my mind right then and there and knew for a fact that I would never flash again. I couldn't. My daughter needed me, and I couldn't let her down. She wrote me a really long letter, telling me all about her life, school, and boyfriend. Wow! It was incredible for me to be reading her actual words. I never experienced that. All I could think about was when I was her age going through school.

I said a prayer right then and there, thanking God for not keeping her from me and thanking Him for letting her reach out to me and not hate me. I was really starting to believe that there just might be a God after all.

I also knew she was at the age where she wanted to know who I was. It was the most incredible feeling I'd ever had, reading that letter. That letter was also the beginning of our relationship. I also made a promise to her that I would be a part of her life and never go back to prison. And there was no way in hell I was going to lie to her.

Epilogue

It won't take much to make me happy. As long as I can stay out of prison and be there for my kids, I'll be the happiest man alive.

I am writing this book from Soledad State Prison in California. I will be released in 2019 at the age of fifty. It's a good age to retire from my addiction. I've had enough. I really have. I want to enjoy the second half of my life because the first half really sucked. I just can't keep coming back to prison. I don't want to grow old and die in here. It's no way to live.

I'm really excited about getting out because I know I'm going to make it out there. I can feel it. I have to do it for my daughter. I have to do it for my son. I have to do it for my mother. I have to do it for everyone who loves me. I have to do it—especially for myself.

I pray every day that my demons will go away, never to return. C'mon, God. I waited fifty years. Show me what you have in store for me. I've stayed strong long enough. Show me you exist; make me a believer.

This is the end of my book, but the beginning of my life. I stayed strong and never gave up hope.

— Patrick Dodenhoff